AMONG THE DEER

AMONG THE DEER
In the Woods and on the Hill
A Stalker Looks Back

DUFF HART-DAVIS

Wood Engravings by Katy Stewart-Smith

Quiller

First published in the UK in 2011
by Quiller, an imprint of Quiller Publishing Ltd

British Library Cataloguing-in-Publication Data
A catalogue record for this book
is available from the British Library

ISBN 978 1 84689 096 3

Printed in Malta by Gutenberg Press Ltd.

Quiller

An imprint of Quiller Publishing Ltd
Wykey House, Wykey, Shrewsbury, SY4 1JA
Tel: 01939 261616 Fax: 01939 261606
E-mail: info@quillerbooks.com
Website: www.countrybooksdirect.com

Contents

1

Call-Out

MY LIFELONG FASCINATION with deer has had some unexpected consequences. One morning when we lived in Oxfordshire a farmer came on the telephone and said abruptly, 'Here – you've got a big rifle, haven't you?'

I didn't know the man, but he was obviously in a state of some agitation, so I agreed cautiously 'Well, yes – why?'

'I need someone to shoot a steer. The blasted thing's gone mad and it's attacking its mates. People, as well.'

'OK,' I said. 'I'll come down. Where are you?'

The farm was only seven or eight miles away, down by the Thames, but such thick fog was lying on the Chilterns and in the river valley that it took me half an hour to nose my way through the lanes. Eventually I arrived at the agreed rendezvous, and found a posse of half a dozen locals waiting by a gate.

'All right,' I said, loading a couple of rounds into the .300 magnum. 'Where is it?'

'Over there.' The farmer pointed vaguely into the fog, and we all started to walk across a grass field – which, being down in the valley, was dead flat. Presently I made out a hedge running across our front, and on our side of it a single, hefty Hereford bullock pacing up and down as if preparing to put in a charge.

'That's him!' said the farmer tensely. 'Why don't you shoot him?'

'Give it a minute,' I said. 'What's beyond the hedge?'

'Nothing.'

'Nothing?'

'Just the village.'

'The village! How far away are the houses?'

'About a hundred yards.'

'Jesus! What about in that direction?' I pointed to the left.

'Nothing that way.'

At that moment I heard the unmistakable noise of a train rattling past in the fog.

'What the hell's *that*, then ?'

'Oh, it's only the embankment.'

'Listen,' I said. 'If I miss, this bullet'll go for two or three miles. We need to get organised.'

After some manoeuvring, I got two men stationed as decoys, one on either side of the rogue animal, against the hedge. Turning back and forth, it could not make up its mind which to charge. By means of hand-signals I moved them inwards until each was about thirty yards from the bullock. I myself shifted to my right until I had it lined up in front of an enormous oak, with a trunk at least four feet wide. Even if I missed the crazed creature, I could hardly miss the tree. I then advanced until the bullock stopped pacing to right and left, and began to fancy me as a potential target. With everyone in position or out of the way, and the animal anchored by indecision, I lay down, took aim and put a bullet into its forehead. Down it went as if poleaxed, and within a couple of minutes it had been borne away hanging by the hocks from the fork lift of a tractor.

The farmer thanked me civilly enough, and I drove slowly home, pleased to have been of service. But the exercise had occcupied most of the morning, and I slightly hoped that in due course some small recompense might appear – perhaps a pound or two of steak. For weeks, for months, nothing materialised, and in the pub I began making jokes about how I'd shot only one steer during the season, but how challenging the assignment had been. Then suddenly there arrived a letter containing a note of thanks, together with a cheque for £25 – a considerable sum, then, and far more than I had earned or deserved. I was left feeling guilty, for I feared that my stories had found their way back to the farmer and caused him to over-react.

2

Born Killer

EVERY MORNING IN term time when I was seven or eight my sister and I would bicycle off across country to catch the school bus, which picked us up at a point on a minor road about a mile from home. For some of the way we were on private estate tracks, but we preferred to take short cuts along woodland rides, even though, in winter, the paths were often so muddy that we had to dismount and push. When we reached the main road, we simply wheeled our bikes into the trunk of a gnarled old beech tree which had been hollowed out by fire. In those carefree days there was no question of any grown-up escorting us, or of us locking up our battered steeds when we left them. Returning in the afternoon, we would pick them up and ride home.

One summer day for some reason I came back on my own, and decided to cut through a wood which lay along the side of a hill. Much of it had once been coppiced hazel, but the bushes had been let go and grown tall, and at the far end they gave way to rough grass-land. As I emerged into the open patch, wheeling my bike, there stood a beautiful animal, broadside-on to me. Its chestnut-coloured coat, strongly marked with white spots, glowed in the sunlight. Legs and throat were white, and sharp little points of antlers protruded from the top of its head. Later I discovered that it must have been a fallow pricket – a second-year buck – of the menil variety, the kind with the strongest markings; but at the time all I knew was that it was a deer.

I was frightened, because the animal was so close, and so much bigger than me. Standing slightly higher up the bank, it looked even taller than it was. Transfixed, I froze and stared at it. For a few seconds the deer stared back at me. Then it wheeled round and bounded off, revealing a black stripe down the centre of its tail. Breathless with excitement, I leapt onto my bike and pedalled furiously for home, desperate to tell my mother what I had seen.

That was the start of a life-long involvement with deer – and for me their magic lay partly in the fact that during the 1940s and 1950s the fallow were rare visitors to the Chiltern woods among which I grew up, so that I had few glimpses of them. Some had broken out of parks during the Second World War, when trees had fallen through walls or fences, and no men had been on hand to repair the damage. The escapers had spread out far and wide over the surrounding hills, and their descendants survived and gradually multiplied in the wild, mainly due to the huge programme of re-afforestation which took place after the war – for the dense new plantations which sprang up everywhere provided them with ideal shelter.

Ignorance about deer was paramount in England at that time. There was no tradition of stalking, as in Germany, where elaborate rules had governed control of big game for centuries. British gamekeepers, foresters and farmers treated deer as vermin, occasionally killing them in shotgun drives – and many went away wounded with a scatter of inadequate pellets lodged in their hide. Others, caught in snares or traps, died wretched, lingering deaths. A note in my gamebook for 25 April 1950, when we were rabbiting, records: 'J. Cook shot at deer in the Heather, and it took a lot of shots to kill it' – an episode all the more deplorable if the animal was a doe and heavily pregnant, as it probably would have been at that time of year.

From some ancestor I had inherited a strong hunting gene. Neither of my parents had it, and to my knowledge my father – the ultimate book-worm – only once fired a shot at a live target. That was on a Boxing Day soon after the war. When a cock pheasant appeared, sitting on the garden fence about thirty yards from the house, the whole family urged him to have a go at it. Food was scarce, and there on top of the ivy-covered palisade sat the makings of a delicious meal, its brilliant plumage gleaming in the sun.

My father reluctantly got out his ancient .22 rifle, left over from Home Guard duties, but he could find only one bullet. While he settled himself on a chair in his bedroom, two of us gently eased the sash window up, and after taking prolonged aim, he fired. *Crack!* The sights of the rifle may well have been awry. The old bullet may have lost power. The gunner may well have been put off by the whispered advice being offered from all sides. Whatever the cause of the fiasco, the sole result of the shot was that a second pheasant jumped up beside the first and sat on the fence crowing.

Young as I was, I found that little episode profoundly disappointing. I wanted my father to get that pheasant. I wanted to smell it cooking, and then eat it. I felt we had botched a golden opportunity.

I was lucky enough to be brought up in a remote farmhouse tucked away in the corner of the Nettlebed Estate – 2500 acres of forest and farmland, to which I had unrestricted access – and to my mother's initial dismay, I turned out to be a born hunter. Later she accepted the fact, but at first she resented the way I abandoned her the moment I got home from school and took off into the woods and fields. My delight was to accompany Harry Brown, the gamekeeper, on his trapping and snaring rounds, and even more to stalk rabbits and pigeons on my own, first with an airgun, then with a single-barrelled 28-bore. In winter, major rabbit-shoots brought tremendous excitement, for I was allowed to go round with Brown the day before, stinking out – that is, dropping empty cartridge cases dipped in a noxious compound called Reynardine into the burrows, to push the rabbits into the open – and then on the day itself to act as a beater.

Because I spent so much time among grown men, I was teased a good deal, not least by a roguish fellow called Jack Cook – the one who shot the deer. Bright of eye and ruddy of cheek, he knew a lot about wildlife and never ceased to instruct me. When I told him I had been hearing a peculiar noise down the wood below our house, and tried to imitate it so that he could identify the source, he immediately said, 'Ah – that's a shrike. Bit like a jay. Hangs his prey up in the hedge. Rare bird, that. You want to get arter 'ee, boy.'

I looked up shrike in my bird book – and sure enough, there was a bird rather like a jay, a carnivore with a strident voice, which impales its food on thorns. Every time I heard the ee-aw noise I rushed down the wood in search of the elusive caller – and only after months of fruitless search did I realise that the sound was coming from a donkey, not in the wood at all, but on the farm the other side of the valley.

My principal associate was Reg Brown, son of the keeper, about my age, and an uncommonly good shot with his little .22. His particular technique was to go quietly up to a patch of brambles, stir the edge of it with his foot and watch intently for any slight tremor of a leaf or twig that would betray the movement of a rabbit. Even if only part of the creature appeared in a gap, he would unerringly pop a bullet into its head.

Some people might have thought me blood-thirsty – but when I was lurking about the woods and hedgerows alone I never wanted to shoot any animal or bird just for the sake of killing it. What I enjoyed was the thrill of pitting my embryonic skills against the highly tuned senses of wild creatures. Without realising it, I was giving rein to an instinct on which, in the distant past, millions of human lives had depended. Shooting for the pot seemed to me the most natural activity on earth, and I became a true country boy, insatiably reading and re-reading the Victorian classics by Richard Jefferies, *The Gamekeeper at Home* and *The Amateur Poacher*, and poring over the books' dark engravings that so strongly evoked a world in which I felt I belonged.

I know that in twenty-first-century Britain the idea of shooting animals – deer, particularly – has become repugnant to a great many people. But to anyone in whom the hunting instinct still burns, it remains an entirely natural activity. To me a deer is a beautiful creature, certainly, but it is also a menace to foresters and farmers, on the increase, and delicious to eat – all good reasons for trying to thin out its ranks and land it in the larder.

3

Amateur Stalker

In time – after school, National Service and university – I
graduated to the pursuit of deer, which by then had become so
much more numerous that they were beginning to cause severe
damage to trees and farm crops. Their increase was reflected in the
sweeping changes which came in with the passing of the Deer Act
(Scotland) in 1959 and the Deer Act (England) of 1963. The new laws
established close seasons and laid down minimum calibres of rifle that
might be used for deer control. Also in 1963 the British Deer Society
was formed with the object of encouraging humane management
and greater respect for deer all round.

I read a good deal about the other species at large in Britain – red,
roe, sika, muntjac and Chinese water deer – but as yet had no experience of them: my first deer were all fallow. The first full-bore rifle I
used was a Rigby .275, borrowed from my godfather Peter Fleming.
This was a weapon with a history, for it had been presented to him by
The Times in 1936 after he had walked 3,500 miles from China to India

– an epic trek – in the company of the formidable Swiss adventurer Ella Maillart, which he recounted in his best-selling book *News from Tartary*. In preliminary despatches to the newspaper he had made jokes about the inadequacy of the only powerful rifle which he had taken with him on the journey – an ancient and unreliable Winchester .44, with which he claimed he could not hit a barn door at forty paces – and after some lively exchanges in the correspondence columns of *The Times* the directors decided that in future he should be decently armed.

Peter never much enjoyed deer-stalking, with the result the rifle had had very little use. It was a fine weapon, nicely balanced but old-fashioned, with no provision for mounting a telescopic sight. Because I found that my left eye was my master eye, I always shot off my left shoulder, and this meant that I had to open and close the action by reaching over and hooking the little finger of my left hand round the knob of the bolt, to pull it up and back. This sounds awkward, but it soon became second nature.

The Mauser action, dating from the 1890s, was thoroughly reliable, but it had one defect in the form of a clumsy safety catch – a lever at the back of the bolt that had to be turned up into a vertical position for 'Safe', and pushed down into a horizontal attitude for 'Fire'. I found that if I did not push it down quite far enough, it would jam the bolt: when I pulled the trigger, there was a tiny click, and the rifle would not go off. But then, the slightest further touch would release the striker, and the rifle would fire when I was no longer aiming correctly.

My first foray as a stalker was so amateurish that I took the .275 out without bothering to zero it on a target. I had heard that a small herd of fallow had taken up residence in a young plantation called Earl's Wood, across the valley from home, and when I went out early one morning, I quite soon found them – six or seven does feeding in line-ahead along the ridge above me, silhouetted on the skyline, only sixty or seventy yards away. I could not distinguish one from another, or tell which was old or young: to my untutored eye they all looked the same.

I am still haunted by the irresponsibility with which I fired at the leader. Beyond the deer lay open country, but a main road and several by-roads ran through it, to say nothing of some public footpaths and bridleways, and I realised that if I missed, the bullet would curve over the top of the hill in a low trajectory and carry on for at least a mile. Even if I hit the target, the odds were that the round would go straight through it. I knew that the shot was inexcusably dangerous – but I was so excited by the proximity of the deer, and so determined to get one of them, that I squeezed the trigger.

Down went the doe as if pole-axed, but then it thrashed about on the ground, and, when it lay still for a moment with its head up, I had to give it the *coup de grace* with another bullet. Going up to it, I found that the first round had struck it about a foot above the point at which I had aimed, and instead of hitting the area of its heart had broken its back. Only when I went on a target later did I find out by experimentation how to align the open sights correctly. What I had done that first time was to hold the rifle so that the tip of the foresight was level with the shoulders of the rear sight, either side of the broad, shallow V. What I *should* have done was to settle the bead of the foresight right in the bottom of the V, and put the bead on the point I wanted the bullet to hit.

That was an unpleasant lesson, which I never forgot; but gradually, as I started stalking, I learnt more about ballistics and ammunition. I found there were two varieties of bullet available for a .275: the 173 grain and the lighter 140 grain, both soft-nosed as required by law, so that they mushroomed on impact and caused maximum shock. The first – the one I used at the outset – was relatively slow, with a velocity of 2300 feet per second and a looping trajectory that made it drop about four inches at a range of one hundred yards, and eight or ten inches at two hundred; the second was faster and flatter, leaving the barrel at 2800 feet per second, and was, I soon realised, just as effective. Not that I ever wanted to engage a live target at two hundred yards: in the woods, the range was more likely to be fifty yards or less.

Another important discovery was that the rifle's trigger pressure could be lowered by a competent gunsmith. When I first used the weapon, the trigger-pull was set at 4½ lbs, which meant (as I said only half in jest) that it needed two men and a winch to make the rifle fire. This in turn made it all too easy to drag the weapon off the target to one side – and sometimes, in the excitement of getting a shot, nerves made it feel as if the trigger was locked, so that it would not pull at all. But with the pressure reduced to a little over 2 lbs, the weapon became easier to shoot and much more accurate.

I was surprised to find that I rarely got a shot lying down. As a cadet at school and then in the army I had done most of my rifle-firing in the prone position; but in woods, and sometimes in fields, trees, undergrowth or crops often blocked the view at ground level, so that I was generally obliged to shoot kneeling or standing. My accuracy improved greatly when I equipped myself with a six-foot bipod which had legs jointed together near the top, so that I could flick them apart at the bottom and steady my rifle on the fork at the upper end.

Besides finding out by trial and error how to stalk and shoot, I had also to master the skills of dealing with carcases. After any successful shot, the immediate necessity (I learnt) was to bleed the deer by severing its jugular vein or plunging a knife into the front of its chest. If this were not done promptly, the blood would congeal in the meat and give it a musty taste, rendering the whole carcase unfit for consumption. The next step was gralloching, also to be done immediately – the removal of stomach and intestines. Mildly disgusting at first, especially if the bullet had burst the stomach, the task became routine as soon as I learnt what all the various organs were – and on frosty winter mornings it was a positive relief to thrust one's hands in among warm entrails. These one could leave on site, discreetly tucked away in a hollow or undergrowth, safe in the knowledge that nature's self-propelled waste-disposal service – foxes, badgers, rats, crows, magpies and other scavengers – would quickly clear them up. Back home in the larder the beast had to be hung up, weighed and prepared for the butcher or game-dealer: head and feet off, heart and lights removed, chest cavity washed out.

Skinning was another skill that I had to acquire by experimentation. I have never forgotten the sight of a neighbouring gardener, whose boss had shot a deer, trying to get its hide off. He was lying on his side on the lawn, with his feet braced against the body, heaving at the skin with both hands and uttering fearful curses. Both he and the carcase were smothered with blood, earth, grit and blades of grass, and he had worked himself into a fine rage. He would have done better by far to hang the beast up by the hocks and pull the skin downwards, starting from the tail end.

It was when I came to butcher a carcase that I first fully realised the value of head- or neck-shots. A chest-shot is deadly, and the safest for a beginner, for the target is efffectively six or eight inches wide and high: even if the bullet misses the heart and hits lungs or liver, it will kill; but even if perfectly placed, it will probably rupture so many bood vessels that both forequarters are ruined: blood seeps through the membranes and invades the muscles, spoiling the joints. A head- or neck-shot – a smaller target, but no less lethal – leaves the main part of the carcase intact; besides, it knocks the deer down on the spot, whereas with a heart-shot, even if a beast is in effect dead on its feet, it may run thirty, forty, even fifty yards before collapsing, and on a winter evening a last charge of that kind, into a thick plantation, can make it very difficult to find.

Equally important, I began to learn the ways of the deer. I found that fallow are highly itinerant, and move around the country in small herds, sometimes only four or five strong, more often in tens or dozens. Being largely nocturnal, they tend to stay in woods during the day, and at last light emerge to graze on farm crops. Often the most effective way to cull them is to intercept them as they start back towards shelter soon after dawn – and to be out on the ground before daylight in winter has always been a magical experience for me. Darkness, silence, the familiar landscape shrouded, air sharp with frost, sky brightening in the east – I always think of A.E. Housman's

> Wake: the silver dusk returning
> Up the beach of darkness brims.

Everything gives me the feeling that I am the first man on earth; and the most thrilling sight of all is of deer coming over the horizon in black silhouette against a crimson glow.

Fallow seem to be photo-sensitive: as the early light strengthens, they become increasingly nervous and head for cover, walking at first, but then trotting and occasionally breaking into a canter. A single, loud whistle may stop them long enough for a rifleman to get off a shot – but he had better be quick, because once on the move they will not hang about for long, and when in the wood, they are even harder to approach.

Deer are tremendous survivors, and equipped by nature with highly efficient senses. Unlike humans, who find it hard if not impossible to remain on the alert for long periods, they maintain their vigilance indefinitely, and without effort. As in India or Africa, where tigers, leopards, cheetahs and lions are a constant threat, in any group of prey species there are always one or two on the look-out for trouble. In Britain the deer seem to know that their only predator is man, and they watch out for him accordingly.

One of their defences is good eye-sight. Opinions differ as to whether or not they are colour-blind, and some scientists believe they can see blue, but no other colours; whatever the truth, except when snow is lying, pale-coloured clothes which reflect light are a giveaway in any British landscape, and it behoves the stalker to dress in drab. But above all, it is movement that attracts a deer's attention. In the woods the temptation for a stalker is always to keep pressing steadily forward in the hope of finding deer; but no matter how cautiously you advance, they almost always see you before you see them. Usually it pays to sit still and wait for them to appear: your eyes, like theirs, will instantly pick up any movement, even the flick of an ear in the middle of a thicket – and if you remain motionless, they will not spot you. On the other hand, they seem able to distinguish the outline of a standing human being from other shapes in the wood: if you move along upright, they are away in a flash; but if you reduce your outline by crouching or crawling, they take alarm far less easily.

The direction of the wind is of paramount importance, for deer have phenomenal scenting powers, and can detect humans at least a quarter of a mile away. One faint touch on the air will make them uneasy, and a strong puff of wind will instantly put them to flight. Such sensitivity means that all stalking operations have to be conducted up-wind, or across it; countless careful approaches have been ruined by the breeze curling treacherously round some feature of the landscape and warning the deer of danger. Scent can also linger on the ground for a surprisingly long time. Once, sitting on the side of a hill, I watched a fallow doe come walking quietly down a grass track across my front in the bottom of a valley: when she reached the point at which I had crossed the path an hour earlier, she leapt into the air and bolted.

Some stalkers – among them that great expert on roe, Richard Prior – believe that deer have a sixth sense which warns them when a human being is dangerously close. I have never noticed this myself. I have been within a few feet of both fallow and red deer, and with the wind blowing from them to me I have escaped detection. High on a Scottish mountainside, on the rocky ground above the heather line, I and a friend were once trying to approach a stag when a little party of three hinds wandered over a ridge and into our line of advance, walking almost straight towards us. Caught in the open, we could do nothing except hug the ground, flatten ourselves among the stones and lie still. The hinds kept stopping to stare at us, bobbing their heads in curiosity, but they never deviated from their course, and they passed within ten feet, having presumably decided that we were nothing but a collection of odd-shaped rocks.

Woodland deer are not only highly alert, but also discriminating. Fallow and roe both differentiate between disturbances that may threaten them and those that are harmless. They will stand still to watch chattering, garishly clad hikers go past along a footpath, because experience has taught them that such groups are not dangerous; but the moment they spot a stalker wreathed in camouflage kit and creeping surreptitiously, they take off.

Similarly, they know the everyday noises of the wood – the keeper coming out in his Land Rover to feed his pheasants, the foresters thinning trees with chain saws – and do not take alarm; but one unexplained crack of a twig a hundred yards away will put them on the alert and probably send them flying. Their hearing is so acute that it pays a stalker to take advantage of any ambient noise, and to use (for instance) the clamour of rooks coming off roost at first light or the drone of a passing aircraft to cover any sound he may make by moving. Except during the rut, when the bucks start calling, fallow make very little noise. Does let off loud, gruff alarm barks if they are suddenly scared, but males rarely give tongue.

Another skill to be mastered is that of tracking. A skilled stalker can glean much information from slots, or footprints, also known as 'sign': what species of animal made them, whether it was male or female, how old it was, whether it was fat or thin, how long ago it passed this way, how fast it was moving, and so on. I myself have always found it difficult to differentiate with certainty between the slots of young fallow does and those of roe: both are about the same size, and roe's hooves are generally more pointed, but often it is hard to be sure. Slots can also be very misleading. I once saw a group of eight mature fallow bucks walk in single file down a grass field and on through a narrow, muddy defile between hawthorn bushes. Just after they had disappeared, I went down to examine their tracks, and from the evidence in the mud I could have sworn that only a single beast had gone through the gap. There was only one large slot to be seen.

As time went by I made some interesting discoveries. One is that deer belong to nobody until they are dead. In law they are classed as neither game nor vermin, but as *ferae naturae* – beasts of wild nature, and become the property of a land-owner only when they are killed on his ground. In winter the prickly leaves of bramble bushes are fallow's favourite food. They also like ivy – always said to be poisonous – and in cold weather eat a good deal of it without taking harm. They know that the hollow beneath the branches of a big yew tree is the warmest place in the wood, and often they stand there, looking out. They prefer to make their own paths through woodland, rather than using man-made tracks or rides, and in hill country they tend to follow the contours, moving along the slopes more than up and down. One speciality of fallow is to create play-rings – points at which young animals dash round and round a mound or an old saw-pit, apparently out of sheer high spirits, creating a circular or oblong track of bared earth.

An effective method of coming to terms with them is to sit up in a high seat, ten or fifteen feet above the ground – a practice much favoured in Germany, where *Hochsitze* are ubiquitous. Being airborne has several advantages. One is that it gives a good view over the surrounding terrain; another that firing down towards the ground is safer than firing horizontally; a third, that deer rarely look up above their own level, so that you do not need much concealment, and a fourth, that the wind will probably carry your scent away over their heads. A high seat is also an ideal platform from which to get a novice a shot. On the ground in a wood, opportunities are usually so fleeting, and the deer so difficult to pick out, that there is no time to explain to a beginner which beast you want him to shoot: by the time you have got him organised, the chance has gone. In a high seat, on the other hand, he should have a clear view, and a wooden or padded steel rail on which to rest his leading wrist, as well as plenty of time to identify the target.

Fallow groupings vary according to the seasons. In mid-winter males and females live together in mixed herds, but in February the bucks tend to separate from the heavily pregnant does and congregate in all-male gangs. In April they cast their old antlers and start to grow new ones – a process which uses up a great deal of energy, and for which there is no certain biological explanation.

Cattle and sheep, in contrast, keep one set of horns for life – so why should deer shed theirs every year? One theory is that rapid growth of new antlers dissipates the excessive testosterone which males build up as they put on condition with good feeding in spring and summer; another, that the annual renewal gives them a chance of replacing their main weapons, should one antler get broken in a fight. Whatever the reason, the growing bone is covered with soft, furry, dark skin known as 'velvet', which is full of blood vessels. When growth is complete, the velvet starts to dry, and the deer clean it off by rubbing on the stems of shrubs or young trees in a process known as 'fraying'. At least the does benefit from this apparent extravagance on nature's part, for they chew up the cast antlers and swallow sizeable lumps, thus ingesting valuable doses of calcium.

Like all other species except Chinese water deer, which have no antlers, fallow bucks grow bigger heads in every succeeding year until they are eight or ten years old; thereafter they are said to be 'going back' as their antlers gradually diminish. Stalkers use the age-old names for bucks as they grow up: in his first year a male is a buck fawn, in his second a pricket, in his third a sorel, in his fourth a sore, in his fifth a bare buck, and at six and afterwards a great buck.

Does remain simply does throughout their lives. In June they give birth to their fawns, often leaving them tucked up in long grass or other vegetation while they feed. Unlike roe, which habitually bear twins, they generally produce one a year. Especially in parks like Richmond, which is alive with members of the public, walkers sometimes make the mistake of thinking that a fawn has been abandoned because they see it lying on its own. To pick one up, or even to touch it, is the worst thing one can do, for the odds are that the infant is in perfect health; but if its returning mother detects human contact, she may well abandon it. The fawns grow at amazing speed, and in three months or so are nearly as tall as their mothers.

The climax of the fallow year comes with the rut in September and October. There is often some mystery about where major bucks spend their summer: for months on end they disappear, putting on weight in sequestered haunts, but then as the weather turns colder they prepare for action by coming down into lower-lying land, wandering along hedges or woodland rides and choosing spots at which they stand thrashing small branches off shrubs or trees with their antlers and scraping at the ground with their forefeet. Even if no one sets eyes on the perpetrators – for they generally come by night – they betray their presence by creating patches of clear earth stippled with footprints and surrounded by a scatter of broken-off leaves and twigs.

For the rut itself, a master buck takes possession of an area which has probably attracted generations of his predecessors. Even though deer rarely live more than fifteen years, some rutting stands are many generations old, and experts differ over what it is that makes such spots so attractive: some believe in the influence of ley-lines, but others maintain that more depends on the texture of the woodland. The deer certainly seem to prefer fairly open areas, with light cover overhead – and if the trees become too dense, or foresters clear too much of the cover, they conduct their business elsewhere.

On his chosen patch, often not much bigger than a tennis court, the master buck parades up and down groaning – that is, giving out loud, guttural grunts. Many a time a startled walker has come hurrying out of a wood with the news that 'there's a bloody great pig in there' – and indeed the noise is like that of a monstrous sow or boar. It sounds as though the buck were snorting through his nose, but in fact the calls issue from a valve in his throat, and he makes them with his mouth wide open, stretching his head and neck upwards as he lets fly.

Deer of all ages answer the summons. Excitement builds as does assemble and mill around, giving out squeaky little calls. Their fawns, now nearly four months old, also swirl about restlessly, infected by the general tension. Lesser bucks lurk and dart round the fringes of the group, on the watch for quick conquests. But the master buck is on the lookout for them: every now and then he scatters them with a sudden charge, and the commotion also sends the does flying. Occasionally the big fellow gets into a real fight, locking antlers with a rival and wrestling so violently that the combatants go crashing sideways through undergrowth until the weaker animal gives way.

The noise and movement step up the pressure still higher – yet it seems to take an age for any doe to be mated. Again and again the buck makes a suggestive approach, but again and again the doe flits out of the way and evades him: no wonder, with so much chasing and fighting, that he may have lost a third of his bodyweight by the time the rut is over – especially as for the past few weeks he has ceased to eat anything except a few mouthfuls of earth.

For the stalker, the mating season brings a good opportunity for taking out injured bucks, or ones of poor quality: there is generally so much movement on a stand that all the participants show themselves sooner or later, and they are so obsessed with procreation that their normal vigilance is much reduced. Even then, culling is by no means easy, especially in the half light of dawn, when the action is often most brisk.

I once took out an experienced red-deer stalker who wanted to witness the fallow rut. Tony, the second Lord Dulverton, was no trophy-hunter; a tremendous expert on red deer, he merely wished to observe how fallow went about their affairs. But I knew that he was an exceptionally good shot, and I told him that if we saw any animal that I thought needed culling, I would ask him to shoot it.

Out we went before dawn on a morning of sharp frost – and there was no shortage of action. Bucks were groaning at various points in the valley, and I could tell from the depth of their voices that several of them were big animals. Their calls seemed to ricochet and echo among the trunks of a mature beechwood. As the light came up we moved quietly in on a stand. We ourselves were in the open, among big trees standing on a clean forest floor, but the deer were darting in and out of a thicket about seventy yards ahead of us. That whole patch of the wood was alive with movement, and every few minutes I got a glimpse of the master buck – a splendid, light-coloured beast, his flanks rippling with condition – as he emerged into the open in pursuit of some female and stood there groaning, with jets of breath condensing in the frosty air. There was no question of shooting him, for he was far too good; but presently I spied a perfect target – a sorel with a deformed, lopsided head, which also appeared briefly every now and then.

'There he is!' I hissed at Tony. 'Shoot the buck on the left.'

'Which one?'

'The dark beast.'

'Tail-on to us?'

'No, no. He's standing broadside.'

'Where?'

'Beside the thick treetrunk.'

'Can't see it.'

Too late. The sorel had vanished – and when this had happened twice more, I took the rifle back and shot the beast myself. At the boom of the discharge the thicket erupted. Fleeing deer burst out of it in a torrent. I had expected to see a dozen or fifteen, but here were twenty, twenty-five, thirty, in a hurtling cavalcade. Yet the maestro was not among them.

'Have you shot the big buck?' Tony asked.

'Not at all. He's in there somewhere. He's just too crafty to show himself.'

Hardly had we stood up and started forward when out he came, a magnificent sight as he cantered off after his harem. In spite of the shock of the rifle shot, his instinct had kept him stationary and hidden until (as he thought) the danger had gone. Afterwards, in a letter of thanks, Tony apologised for his failure to spot the sorel when I told him to fire. He had very much enjoyed the morning, he wrote, but his attempt to single out the right target had been 'like trying to shoot a ballet dancer while looking through a kaleidoscope in a theatre with most of the lights turned out.' That and other similar experiences gradually taught me how cunning senior bucks can be, and I realised that it is mainly sheer guile which enables them to survive for ten or twelve years.

My own early ignorance was more than matched by that of some town dwellers. I once took out a senior business executive who, as we were creeping through a wood in the dawn light of a frosty October morning, tapped me on the shoulder and whispered, 'What do they do if they see us coming? Do they lie down and bury themselves in leaves?'

'Yes,' I told him. 'That's exactly what they do – so if ever you see leaves going up in a fountain, let me know.'

His grasp of country matters was rivalled only by that of a woman from Essex who rented a holiday cottage in Worcestershire, but abandoned it after a single day. In a letter of explanation she told the estate agent, 'The property was fine, *but we had to leave* [my italics]. I hated the way the sheep kept staring at me, and I thought the lavatorial habits of the cattle were disgusting.'

Since woodland stalking is mostly, by its very nature, crepuscular, one rarely meets anybody else – and only once in my entire career have I been intercepted while recovering a shot beast. This is not because I behave surreptitiously, but because I operate mainly at dawn and dusk, when few people are abroad. On that one occasion, however, I had shot a fallow doe at first light, and left it, gralloched, in the middle of a stubble field. When I went back to collect it at about 9am, I was just loading it into my jeep when I heard a drumming of hooves, rapidly growing louder, and up galloped a decidedly attractive woman on a piebald horse.

'Who the hell are you?' she demanded.

I told her and countered: 'Who are *you*?'

It turned out that she was the wife of the new farm manager, recently arrived, and nobody had told her that I would be around. But that, as I say, was the only time I have been caught in possession of a body, and the encounter ended amicably.

4

Loch Choire

IN THE AUTUMN OF 1963 my parents-in-law, John and Diana Barstow, took the lease of Loch Choire (pronounced 'Core'), a deer forest in Sutherland, and with characteristic generosity invited friends and members of their family to join them there for a week or two. Never having been to the Scottish Highlands, I had only a faint idea of what the place might be like, but I was excited by the idea of stalking in an entirely different environment, particularly as it was so far to the north.

The journey alone was something of an epic. Only the first section of the M1 had then been completed, from St Albans to Birmingham, and for a motorist heading north out of London only the first part of that was any use. Thereafter it was a question of weaving one's way through town after town, city after city, driving through the night and into the next morning. At the time our family transport was a pale blue minivan, which (as anybody who owned one will remember) was very low-slung and had minimal springing.

For some reason my wife Phylla (short for Phyllida) had to stay behind for a day, and then fly up to Wick to join the party. Thus I was faced with a marathon drive on my own. Details of my progress have mercifully faded – except that at about four in the morning I failed to notice that in one of the Highland towns through which I passed – perhaps Pitlochry – the road had been dug up. Without noticing the temporary barriers, I suddenly dropped at least a foot into an excavated area floored with rubble. The impact, combined with fright, woke me up thoroughly, and I pressed on.

By the time I had cleared Inverness, with three hours still to go, I was hardly in a state to appreciate the scenery of Scotland's north-east coast; but spirits revived when at last I turned inland at Helmsdale and went up the single-track road that follows the celebrated salmon river, with the sinuous strath growing ever wilder and more desolate.

Excitement mounted as I reached Kinbrace, a one-horse halt on the railway, and turned westwards into the hinterland. Huge sweeps of dun-coloured moor stretched away on either side of the road, without a house in sight, and on that fine morning dove-grey cloud-shadows were sliding softly and silently across the empty land. Four miles on I came to a little cluster of buildings, painted white and green, which I identified from the map as Badanloch Lodge.

There I turned left off the main road and bounced down a rough gravel track which swung round the end of a great sheet of water and over a dam equipped with sluices, through which the beginning of the Helmsdale river was flowing. For eleven more miles I bumped and rattled along that spine-shaking approach, with low hills rising on my left, lochs lying in the flats to the right, and far ahead on the western horizon the great summits of Ben Hee, Ben Hope and the turreted Ben Loyal standing out magnificently against the sky.

The further I went, the higher the hills on the left became, and when at last I swung left-handed round the end of them, nearly seven hundred miles from home, there in front of me stood the lodge. Since I had approached it from the back, I could not appreciate the splendour of its position until I looked out of the front windows. From them a tremendous view opened up to the south-west. Starting below the house, Loch Choire itself stretched away for more than three miles, and beyond it in the distance another narrow sheet of water extended on the same line for another mile and a half towards a rocky, V-shaped pass in the skyline. For the whole of their joint length the lochs were cradled on both sides by majestic hills, rising on the right to the summit of Ben Klibreck, over 3000 feet high. In all the 33,000 acres of the property there was only one other house in sight – a little white cottage across the near end of the loch – and apart from a couple of small plantations along the shore, the prospect was utterly barren: a wilderness of bog, grass, heather and rock.

The grandeur of the landscape, its emptiness, the steepness of the hills, the tremendous views – all this made my heart pound. The beauty of the place was bewitching, especially on that first quiet morning, when the surface of the loch lay still as a sheet of glass, reflecting hills, sky and clouds like a gigantic mirror. I quickly conceived a particular love of the Klibreck range, the half of the forest on the north side of the water, where a line of hills steadily increases in height and splendour as it runs from north-east to south-west, from the modest Corrie Feuran, where the remains of old sheilings (pastures) are still evident, through Rowantree Hill, the Whip and Meall Ailein (Allan's Hill) to Meall nan Con (Hill of the Dogs) and the isolated summit of Klibreck itself.

My immediate instinct was to head for the high ground – and this I began to do soon enough, as two stalking parties were going out every day, each to shoot one stag; and even though the golden chance to be the rifle came but rarely, followers were always welcome, since man-power was usually needed to pull a shot beast to a point at which it could be loaded onto a pony or into a boat. Fit young pullers were always welcome – and as I enjoyed strenuous exercise, I was cut out for the role.

Even though I had equipped myself with a reasonably good pair of binoculars, at first I had trouble spotting the deer at all. Then, after a day or two, tutored by Colin McKay, the experienced second stalker, I began to see them without having to ask him for pointers. If they were on a skyline, it was easy, for they stood out against the sky; much more often, a herd showed only as a group of tiny, rust-brown dots, a warmer colour than the grass or heather in which they were lying on the face of a hill. I soon learnt how sheer distance can defeat the eye. To begin with, I presumed that if there were deer in direct line of sight, I would see them. Then I realised that the amount of information reaching the naked eye from a couple of miles away is often too small for the brain to interpret, and that only binoculars or a telescope can give an accurate idea of what lies ahead.

Another surprise was the poverty of the vegetation. Not only was ninety-nine per cent of the ground bare of trees, most of the low ground was covered with inedibly coarse grass, of no use to herbivores, or even with rushes and delicious-smelling but equally useless bog myrtle. On many stretches tussocks with invisible deep holes between them made the going difficult. Higher up the slopes there was some heather, with pockets of good grass dotted about in the hollows; above that was arctic tundra of very short dry grass strewn with stones, and above that again great fields of shattered rock. In the whole huge estate there was pathetically little good grazing for the deer. The heathery areas were inhabited by a few grouse, but the ground above 2000 feet was the domain of the ptarmigan, and of the golden eagle and the peregrine which hunted them.

Every morning two small stalking parties set off from the lodge at about nine o'clock. The Head Stalker, George McNichol, was nearing the end of his active career and was impeded by an arthritic hip. 'Ma hup is always on ma mind,' he would say – but still he often started out up the Eagle Face path, which climbed steeply behind the house. The other party might go up the loch by boat, propelled by an outboard motor, to land half-way along the northern shore and stalk on Klibreck, or putter on to the head of the loch and walk up Corrie-na-Fearn, the grand valley which curled away to the south-west from the water's end. Behind the stalkers, ghillies led out the sturdy garrons – the ponies which brought stags down – and sometimes, if the professionals had a day off, members of the family party would be pressed into service as pony-boys or -girls.

On fine days the role of pony-boy was agreeable enough. One could bask in the sun for long periods, keeping an eye on the stalkers' movements with binoculars; but if one fell asleep for a few minutes, and woke to find that the group of tiny figures had disappeared, one had nerve-racking moments trying to decide whether to move on or stay put. Nor was it easy to interpret signals. Before the advent of walkie-talkie radios, a small plume of smoke rising from the heather almost certainly meant that they had got a stag, and that one should start bringing the pony to the base of the hill; but a handkerchief waving was more difficult to see, let alone to interpret. Of course, when rain was lashing down, waiting around for hours was misery, and the ordeal could be even worse in still, muggy weather, when the midges came out in force.

Familiar as I was with deer in the south, I now had everything to learn – not least that the scale on which operations took place was far greater than anything I had tried at home. Some elements were the same: we had to move into the wind, or across it, keeping down-wind of any deer we were trying to approach. Similarly, we had to keep out of sight as much as possible, or, if in view, move like snails.

Tactics, however, were completely different. A single stalk could last all day, especially when the wind was fickle. Colin would spot stags at a great distance – maybe a couple of miles – and if they were in a commanding position, we might have to make a huge detour to come in above or below them on the face where they were lying. All too often it turned out that groups of hinds were lying or feeding between us and the stags, and if the hinds saw us and started to run, they would put the stags away. It struck me that stalking on the open hill was like playing billiards on a gigantic scale: any false move could set off one herd, and that lot in turn would start another lot going with a long-range bounce, like a giant cannon. A moment or two of carelessness on our part could clear an entire hill. I also saw that far more actual stalking was required here than in the woods: without any trees for cover, we were constantly seeking out dead ground, crawling across open spaces, creeping up shallow gullies and, in the final stages of an approach, worming our way forward with infinite care, belly-down in the grass, heather, peat or (worst of all) water.

Nobody (to my knowledge) has described the stalker's movements more felicitously than the eighteenth-century poet Duncan Ban Mac-Intyre, an illiterate forester who recited his poems to a clergyman (here translated from the Gaelic by Professor J. S. Blackie):

> The hind that dwelleth in the glen
>   Is light of foot and airy;
> Who tracks her way upon the Ben
>   Must be full wise and wary.
>
> Softly, softly on her traces
> He must steel with noiseless paces,
>   Nigh and still more nigh,
> Lest she turn with sudden starting
> And, like feathered arrow darting,
>   Cheat the eager eye.
>
> He must know to dodge behind
> Rock and block in face of wind;
> In the ditch and in the pit
> Dripping lie and soaking sit,
>   Stoop and creep and crawl,
> Ever with quick eye to note
> Face of earth, and clouds that float
>   In the azure hall.

In September we were not shooting hinds, but it was often they who gave us most trouble, simply by being in the way, and always on guard. Many an old hind had perfected a particular trick: if she caught a glimpse of something she did not like, she would stare at it with her

head up for a minute or two, and then resume – or pretend to resume
– grazing … only to whip her head up again a moment later, and keep
repeating the process – down, up … down, up – hoping to verify her
suspicion, in a cervine version of granny's footsteps. This habit meant
that, once we had caused even the faintest alert, we had to be extra-
careful not to show ourselves again. I found that different stalkers had
different methods of trying to allay suspicion: one, if spotted, would
sink down on to his knees with infinite slowness, millimetres at a time,
until he was out of sight, but another would drop as abruptly as if he
had been shot, thus vanishing from the deer's field of view as rapidly
as possible.

At Loch Choire the local men had wonderful Sutherland accents,
which turned a word like 'hill' into something between 'hell' and
'hull', and 'back' into 'barck'. Colin had a habit of plucking off the
soft, white heads of cotton grass as he walked until he had a whole
collection in his jacket pocket. Then, as we drew near deer, he would
release little tufts, one by one, so that they floated away over the hill
and showed him the precise direction of the wind.

Mist was always an enemy, for on any high ground it brought operations to a halt. If we could not see what was in front of us, there was
no point in moving forward, for the odds were that we would either
bump into deer, which would see us just as we saw them, and take off
into the wind, perhaps causing an unseen shunt and clearing the
entire hill without us knowing what had happened. Also, mist could
be thoroughly disorientating. One day, enveloped by cloud on the
steep side of a corrie, we sat down to wait for the air to clear, and after
a while I went briefly to sleep, lying back on the springy heather.
When I next opened my eyes, I was amazed to see an immense silver
disc shining (as I thought) in the sky above me, and I leapt to my feet
with a cry of 'Flying saucers!' In fact what had appeared through a gap
in the mist was the top end of the loch, bounded by its curved, sandy
beach, and I was seeing acres of water rather than metal. Having lost
my vertical bearings as well as my horizontal ones, I thought the
apparition was in the sky above me.

One unwelcome surprise was the power of that barely visible menace, the Highland midge. Physically minute, but capable of causing incredible irritation, *Culicoides impunctatus* is a curse to stalkers, fishermen, hikers and campers alike. Tiny though they are, midges are complex insects, and they attack humans because they are attracted by the carbon dioxide which all living creatures exhale. Living in damp, peaty places, where they feed on dead plant material, they take to the air in dense swarms whenever the weather is suitably still and moist, and drive you to distraction if you are lying in wait for a stag to rise or attempting some intricate operation like adjusting a rifle sight or tying a fly. Over the years numerous patent repellents have been put on the market, but none is wholly effective, and the only way to preserve your head and face intact is to wear a veil or net over a hat – something I have always found impossibly claustrophobic.

When I once asked a stalker how long midges live, he replied explosively, 'TOO LONG!' – and in fact they survive for several summer months. Females must feed on blood to ensure that their eggs will hatch, and when they bite, they inject saliva which causes an allergic reaction. In most people this is merely annoying, but for some it can be positively dangerous. One certain fact is that midges cannot navigate in wind, and if a breeze is blowing at more than four or five miles per hour, they stay down in the grass or reeds. In the autumn millions are killed off by frost, but their larvae burrow into wet ground and survive there until they hatch out in the spring.

It was a joy to find that the Highland environment has a nomenclature all its own. Stalking parties go not 'up the hill' or 'into the hills', but just 'to the hill', and once they are up, they are 'on the hill'. A stream is a burn; a valley with one closed end, a corrie; a bigger valley, usually with a river in it, a glen; the boundary between one estate and another is the march. Every prominent feature of the landscape has a Gaelic name, usually descriptive of its appearance – Carn Dearg, the Red Summit, Meall Odhar, the Yellow Hill, Sgurr-na-Ciche, the Bosom Peak, and so on. The sandwich and bar of chocolate which one takes along to stave off hunger is not one's lunch, but one's piece. Female red deer are hinds rather than does, their offspring calves rather than fawns.

Like fallow bucks, the stags grow larger antlers every year until the age of eight or nine; a second-year beast is known as a spiker (the equivalent of a pricket), but after that there are no gradations like sore and sorel to mark intermediate years. Mature stags are judged largely on the number of points they carry: a beast with twelve points is a Royal, and one with fourteen (very rare in the Highlands) an Imperial. A stag whose antlers end in single points, with no forks, is a switch, and always a prime target, because if he gets into a fight during the rut, his antlers will not lock with those of his adversary: instead, they are liable to slide through an opponent's guard and deal him a fatal stab in the ribs. Finally, a stag with no antlers at all is a hummel, to be culled if possible, as an undesirable freak – although no one knows for certain whether one hummel will breed another and pass on his genetic eccentricity.

I saw straight away that red deer are taller and more rangy than fallow. What I took time to appreciate was that the Highland animals of today are but shadows of their distant ancestors, which were far larger and heavier. Remains discovered in peat bogs show that the red deer of antiquity were half as tall again and probably twice as heavy, because their environment was much more benign, and they had far better shelter in the great Caledonian forest of antiquity. Today a hill stag brought into the larder weighing sixteen stone is considered a good beast, but red deer living in woodland often reach twenty-five stone or more – and clearly the primeval stags were at least that weight.

Loch Choire lodge was, and is, a splendid building, combining style and squalor in typical Highland fashion. The earliest version of it was created during the 1880s by that redoubtable stalker Henry Chaplin, who, in spite of his tremendous bulk – in the south all his hunters had to be able to carry nineteen stone – rented more than 70,000 acres from the Duke of Sutherland.

Finding only a shepherd's hut on an this outstanding site, Chaplin constructed the first lodge, and the building was later extended, with improvements in ducal style. The front rooms, facing down the loch, were finely panelled, the sitting-room made particularly comfortable and elegant, with a wide bow window commanding the view. The duke's bedroom, above it, had the same noble dimensions and pine panelling, and the duke's bath was a wonder on its own, being seven feet long and more than two feet deep. The back of the building, clad in corrugated iron and painted green, was another matter: a primitive kitchen, boiler-room, boot-room and game-larder occupied the ground floor, and upstairs was a maze of small 'motor-men's rooms', with walls and ceilings of tongue-and-groove pine panelling.

In all the main rooms and corridors mounted trophies sprouted from the walls – not just antlers, but whole stuffed stags' heads, whose glass eyes gleamed in the flickering electric light produced by a generator. Giant trout in glass cases constituted a further hazard for visitors with nervous dispositions, especially after the generator had shut down at midnight, and nocturnal expeditions to one or other of the numerous bathrooms had to be conducted by torchlight. Water was heated by a gigantic, old-fashioned boiler known as Moloch (after the heathen god or monster reputed to consume everything offered to it), and baths were generally hot, but the water emerging from the taps was the colour of well-brewed tea, since it came straight off the hill and was full of peat. Drinking water was at least filtered, but it too was of dubious quality, as a deer or a sheep might well have died in the burn from which it came. In the 1960s there was no telephone, but communication with the general store at Kinbrace, on the railway line, could sometimes be achieved through an unreliable radio link, which functioned for one short period in the morning and another in the evening.

Life in the lodge was highly convivial. Huge breakfasts were quickly followed by the making of pieces. How much was one going to want in the middle of the day? Whatever you chose – a couple of sandwiches, a slice of cake, a bar of chocolate, an apple – you could be certain that after you had sat or lain or crawled on it a few times, or immersed it in water, the contents of the little packet would have been compressed into a single, homogeneous mass.

Next came target practice for those who were to shoot that day. In theory every rifleman was supposed to engage a proper target, firing across one corner of the bay at a board beside the stag larder, while one of the stalkers spotted the strike of his shots with a telescope; but often the midges on the firing-point were so pestilential that a quick blast at a patch of lichen on a rock was reckoned good enough. When a puff of dust and splinters flew off the surface, the stalkers were inclined to say, 'Och, that's fine' – but in fact the bullet might have struck six inches or more from the point of aim.

The stag larder was a place best avoided, for in those days its facilities were primitive, to say the least, and especially in warm weather it generated astoundingly noisome smells. Latter-day hygiene police – had they existed, and had they survived the shock of inspecting it – would certainly have ordered its immediate closure. It was no surprise to hear that the price paid for venison remained very low, for much of the output from Highland forests was poorly handled and took far too long to reach processing plants. We heard stories of how some keepers and ghillies threw newly shot stags into the loch and floated them down to the other end, so that the sodden carcases would gain weight and become more valuable. Yet things must have been even worse in Victorian days, before the advent of motor transport, when a horse-drawn wagon used to make its laborious way up from Golspie once a week to collect carcases, some of which were already turning green.

Nine o'clock saw the departure of our stalking parties, but fishermen and women could afford more leisurely starts before setting out to try for salmon on the River Mallart (which runs out of Loch Choire on its way to join the Naver) or trolling for trout on one of the lochs. There were always fish in the Mallart, but if the river was low, it was almost impossible to make them take a fly, and less scrupulous fishermen would resort to spinning or, in very high water, to worms. Loch

Choire itself, always known just as 'the loch', was always good for a few trout, especially at the top end, where burns ran into it from Loch a'Bheallaich (to us the Top Loch) and from the wonderfully distant Corrie-na-Fearn. But parties venturing that far needed to watch the weather, for if a northerly wind blew up during the day, substantial waves would build up on the loch, so that they might find it impossible to boat back, and be faced with a four-mile trudge home.

The stuffed leviathans in the Lodge proved that Loch Choire did harbour, or had harboured, very large trout, almost certainly cannibals, and we resorted to all sorts of tricks trying to catch them. Supposing that they inhabited the murky depths, and that we might rouse them up with flashers, we cut the lids out of biscuit tins, fitted them with swivels, sank them with weights and towed them for miles behind the boats – all to no avail. Easily the most reliable and prolific souce of fish was Truderscaig, a triangular and relatively shallow loch lying in the low ground half a mile below the approach road, which sometimes yielded fifty trout in a day.

As dark was falling the party would reassemble for tea, baths, a snooze, a dram and then a gargantuan dinner, prepared by girls (often New Zealanders) hired for the duration, the meal marred only by the thought of the washing-up, in which all except senior citizens were expected to take part. An occasional shriek, followed by the crash of falling crockery, would betray the fact that one of the young bucks had taken to rutting in the kitchen.

My first stag, which I shot with Colin, is still fresh in my memory. Our purpose, as always, was to find a mature beast with a heavy body, rather than to shoot a royal, or any animal with a good or promising head. Best of all would be a hefty switch, next best a big old stag that was going back.

My day as the rifle was gloomy and wet, with spells of drizzle drifting in from the west, heavy enough to blur our binoculars whenever we tried to use them. In the morning we made our way up into Corrie Ba – a huge bowl stretching back a couple of miles into the heart of the Klibreck range – and we had one breath-taking stalk, when we crawled in on a group of stags grazing slowly along a high face. It was sheer bad luck, and through no mistake on Colin's part, that they kept moving on, tails towards us, and that none of them presented a target as they disappeared over a ridge, enticingly huge on the skyline. For various reasons, mainly the direction of the wind, it was impossible to go after them, so we sat down to eat our piece and make a new plan.

In the afternoon it came on to rain more persistently. We walked and walked without finding any other worthwhile target, and when we started to head for home, with the light already fading, my spirits sank. I was tired and wet, and feared we had run out of options. Then suddenly, as we worked our way left-handed round a huge, smooth shoulder, Colin spotted movement down to our right, a couple of hundred yards beneath us. He dropped on one knee as if shot, then slowly came upright again. Binoculars confirmed that a party of eight or ten mature stags was walking round the hill in the same direction as us, but because of the curvature of the ground, we could see only their antlers, moving briskly in single file.

'Quick!' whispered Colin. 'We'll cut them off.'

We climbed a few feet, which put us out of the deer's view, and then doubled forward round the contour over the short, springy turf. After three or four hundred yards Colin turned downhill, scuttled a few more yards and went into a crouch.

'Get ready,' he panted, handing me the Rigby. 'They'll be here directly.'

The stags were coming round below us from our right. The only way I could aim in their direction was by sitting on the ground with elbows braced on knees – by no means a comfortable or steady position. I just had time to think, 'This is *not* what I was hoping for,' when the posse came into view – antlers first, then heads and necks, then bodies. Colin scrutinised them quickly, then said, 'Second from the back. When he stops, take him.'

I had been hoping for a target like Landseer's Monarch of the Glen, huge, highly coloured, beautifully illuminated and poised majestically on the horizon against sky and more distant hills. Instead, I was being asked to fire in murky light at a black creature that looked the size of a goat, against a background of mist and rain – *and it was moving*.

Before I could remonstrate, Colin gave a sharp whistle. The stags stopped. Mine was standing clear, broadside on, and Colin hissed urgently, '*Take him now!*'

My hands were shaking as I turned down the lever of the safety catch, which was slippery with rain. Summoning maximum effort to hold the rifle steady, I put the bead of the foresight on the point where I thought the heart would be and squeezed the trigger.

I heard the thump as the bullet struck, and Colin snapped, 'It's into him!' but the whole bunch of stags went off at a gallop and in a couple of seconds had disappeared round the contour. Colin grabbed the rifle, slid another round into the breech and set off fast downhill, angling towards the point at which the deer had vanished. In a few moments he slowed to a walk and moved on more cautiously, pausing before he peered over every little ledge. At last he stopped, looked round and with a grin on his face said, 'He's fine!'

The stag lay on its back in a little gulley between rocks, all four feet in the air. My bullet had flown straight enough and had hit slightly low. But, as Colin said, the stag had been dead on its feet from the moment of impact, and only reaction had propelled it that far. I realised I should have aimed slightly higher, to compensate for the steep downhill angle; but I felt immensely relieved. Colin quickly bled the beast and smeared blood on my cheeks and forehead, warning me, 'Ye'll no take that off till morning!' But in fact the rain was coming down so hard that by the time we reached the low ground, my face had been washed clean.

Our pony-man had been observing our progress through binoculars from the loch-side, and he came across towards the bottom of the hill as we dragged the beast down. To make sure that the pony did not move while the stag was being loaded, he took off his jacket and draped it over the animal's head, tying the arms loosely under its neck in a secure blindfold. He and Colin adjusted the girth of the saddle and then, with stag on board, tightened all the leather straps, black with age, that held it firm, with its head twisted back over its shoulder so as to keep its weight central. We had a long walk back to the lodge, but somehow my tiredness had vanished.

That first year we had arrived at Loch Choire in the middle of September, and we were there on the 20th, known as 'The Day of the Roaring', which marks the traditional start of the rut. Sure enough, as the nights grew colder we began to hear single roars echoing out from rocky faces – long, low bellows like those of cattle. The stags were still in their all-male herds, but one by one they started to turn black as they freshened up for action by wallowing in peat hags into which they had urinated.

Colin explained that most of the stags in the neighbourhood spent the summer on Loch Choire's high ground, where they were less troubled by flies and midges than they would have been lower down; but that, come the rut, they would 'break out' and go down to the neighbouring forests of Borrobol, Ben Armine and Dalnessie in search of hinds. One day, out towards the Ben Armine march, we looked down on an amazing sight: stags in a great mass were charging in one direction for a few hundred yards, stopping abruptly, and then galloping wildly back to the point from which they had started. They were not frightened – merely excited. There must have been five hundred of them, making what one of the ghillies called 'this dirty race', preparing to break out. It was a fantastic spectacle, but also a slightly depressing one, for it meant that we were about to lose the main body of our stags, and that stalkers on other forests, who might be less selective than us, would get a chance to shoot them.

Day by day the rut gathered pace. The stag parties split up, and individual beasts began to roar defiance as they marshalled harems of hinds, much as the fallow did in the south – except that here everything took place in the open. As at home, the deer became easier to approach because they were so preoccupied with their own affairs.

Fights between rivals broke out with increasing frequency, and master stags began using a different call: a series of staccato grunts – *Uh! Uh! Uh! Uh!* – which clearly said *You – eff – off – for – a – start* – when they wanted to be rid of some interloper. Losers would either skulk on the fringes of the group, or make off at a trot across the hill in search of better things; and these wanderers, known as travelling stags, would sometimes come straight towards us if we lay still. Altogether, the rut was a tremendous spectacle, and a wonderful time to be on the hill.

We were so enthralled by our first experience of the Highlands that we returned to Loch Choire year after year, courtesy of my parents-in-law, and I gradually got to know the ground better. Greater familiarity brought home how tremendously remote the lodge must have seemed in Chaplin's day. In the 1880s, apart from the track leading in, there were no roads or even pony paths; if the stalkers killed a stag at the far end of the estate, they would leave it on the hill until morning, and then send out ghillies with a pony to bring it in. Once the stag was loaded and strapped on to the deer saddle, the horse would often be turned loose, to pick its own way home, which it did with unerring skill, back-tracking the route of its outward journey and avoiding the numerous bogs along the way.

Things became easier in the late nineteenth and early twentieth centuries, when either Chaplin or the Duke put in a pony-path round the Loch, and an extension of it that struck past the Top Loch to the pass and on over to the Crask Inn on the main road to Tongue. Another path opened up Corrie-na-Fearn, and the Eagle Face path led over the high ground to Ben Armine, the Sutherlands' next lodge, nine miles away to the south-east.

Half-way across, a substantial wooden shelter known as the Shel-lachan Stable was built in a sheltered spot beside a burn. The name may derive from *sealga*, the hunter, and here in the old days men with fresh horses had been stationed throughout the summer and autumn, in case they were suddenly needed for stalking operations.

The path was so well engineered, and so carefully surfaced and maintained, that the Duke had been able to ride from one lodge to another in less than an hour. Wherever one of the paths crossed a burn of any size, the builders had created a shod ford with neatly cut blocks of stone, and many of these cobbled pavements survive to this day.

For several years I persisted with my borrowed .275, learning all the time about how the rifle performed at various ranges. At first, in my ignorance, I had supposed that it was somehow unsporting to rest the weapon or one's leading wrist on anything solid; but I soon realised that this was a ridiculous notion, and that it was far better to have the rifle firmly bedded, provided the barrel was not touching rock or any other hard surface, which would make the bullet fly high. Soon I took to carrying a small satchel, and this made a comfortable rest when stuffed with my piece and a spare jersey.

Stalking with Colin in Corrie Crask, at the southern end of the forest, I got a salutary lesson in the use of open sights. Having crawled in on a shootable stag, we found we could get no closer than 200 yards – a long shot, but feasible, since I had a good position. We therefore decided to give it a try, and after taking careful aim, I fired.

'You're under!' Colin snapped. 'Fire again.'

The stag ran forward a few paces, but was evidently confused about where the shot had come from, and again stood broadside. Something told me to push up the little flap on the rear sight which said '200 yds'. The difference seemed infinitesimal, but when I took the same aim and fired again, I hit the beast in the heart.

That one experience should have taught me to be wary of using weapons with which I was not familiar; but when Phylla's uncle Harold Caccia, who had been British Ambassador in Vienna and had done much stalking in the Alps, produced an Austrian rifle with a telescopic sight, I gratefully accepted his suggestion that I should take it on the hill. Before we set forth I fired two shots at a target at a range of one hundred yards. Both hit the centre of the bull, almost touching each other, and Colin was so delighted that he announced jubilantly, 'No stalk today! Shoot from quarter of a mile! Shoot from half a mile!'

In the event I shot from about two hundred yards, which proved a lot too far. Because the mist was down on the hill, we went out on the low ground below the road, where the only cover was the occasional small mound, and we stalked a bunch of stags lying on one of the little braes. After much crawling back and forth, and trying different approaches, we could get no nearer, and lay in a firing position, waiting for the stags to rise. When they did, I took careful aim, putting the cross-hairs of the sight half-way up the shoulder of a stag which was standing not quite broadside, but facing slightly in our direction. To my dismay, the bullet broke both its front legs just above the knee, and for a minute or two it lurched about horribly on the stumps before, aiming higher, I finished it with another round. Later, back on the target, we found that although the rifle was correctly zeroed at one hundred yards, it was dropping a foot at 200 – something we should have taken the trouble to discover before we went out.

At Loch Choire itself there was never any shortage of outdoor enter-tainment; anyone not stalking could fish, or walk up grouse, of which there were enough to make tramping through the heather worth-while. We occasionally hired a pointer for the day, which made the exercise much more interesting and rewarding. A still more demand-ing physical challenge was to scale the heights for ptarmigan, which live on or above the 2000-foot contour. Charming birds, resembling speckled grey grouse, they were so tame on some days that they would toddle along in front of us, or sit about in the rocks giving out their whirring, creaking calls, like the noise of rusty barn-door hinges opening; but at other times they were so wild that the instant we appeared they would go spinning out over the glen in a whirl of white wings, often prescribing a huge semicircle before coming back in to land on the same hill. When I once asked a ghillie what ptarmigan live on, he replied, 'Stones, mostly', and although he was joking (knowing that they eat heather shoots and various berries) he made the point that their environment is extraordinarily harsh.

A day on the ptarmigan ground was made memorable if we managed to visit the spring known as Klibreck Wells, where ice-cold water, as fresh and clear as on the day of creation, bubbles out of the ground into a tiny basin ringed by brilliant green moss, in the middle of the last smooth slope that leads to the summit. From the very high ground we could see down into the Sanctuary, a corrie with such spectacularly steep flanks that no beast could be extracted from it. Hence its name: when the deer went into it, they were safe, for nobody ever stalked within its daunting confines.

It was on the back of Klibreck that I once had a startling encounter. Late in the afternoon, picking my way between house-sized rocks as the sun was setting, I came round a corner and found myself confronting what I took to be a gate-post some three feet high and a foot wide, with a tapering top, standing upright about ten yards ahead. I just had time to think, 'What a hell of a place for anyone to put in a gate-post!' when the top of the brown pillar moved. The roosting golden eagle spun its head round, gave me a disdainful glare, spread its eight-foot wings and went sailing out over the glen. As I looked over the domain of the great predator, with far summits glowing in the evening sun, there rose in my mind Robert Louis Stevenson's poem, 'In the Highlands, in the country places', in which he longs to revisit his old haunts,

> Where the old red hills are bird-enchanted –
> Lo! For there, among the flowers and grasses
> Only the mightier movement sounds and passes;
> Only winds and rivers,
> Life and death.

Inevitably, stalking holidays were occasionally marred by mishaps. One evening, as we got ready for dinner, we realised belatedly that several of the party, including my mother-in-law Diana, had not come in from a fishing expedition on which they had set out up the loch several hours earlier. We had already had baths, changed into tidy clothes and put away the odd dram, so we felt disinclined to go out into the night, which was very wild, with a westerly gale blowing up. But as the minutes ticked away, our uneasiness increased, and we were further provoked by the neurotic behaviour of that year's cook – not, for once, a girl, but a middle-aged woman, who at about 8.45 announced that the venison was ruined, and then at 9 pm that she was leaving in the morning (how she proposed to do this was not clear, as she had no transport of her own).

Galvanised into action at last, we pulled rough clothes back on, launched one of the small, open fishing boats and set off up the loch across the full blast of the wind, with spray exploding over the starboard bow. What with the roar of the gale and the noise of the outboard engine running, we could hear nothing, so every couple of minutes we shut down the motor, yelled as loud as we could and swept the scudding black waves with a torch beam. Then, as we began to be blown backwards, we started up again and forged ahead a bit more.

Rapidly sobering up, we repeated the sequence three or four times without evoking any response; but then, at the next attempt, my torch picked up an answering flash in the middle of the water, and when we doused our engine again, the sound of a dog barking came faintly through the wind. Sweeping the beam once more, I picked up a pair of eyes, and then the pale form of Lucy, my mother-in-law's yellow Labrador, standing in the bows of the other boat, barking like a mad thing. In a few moments we were alongside, to discover that the crew had run aground and smashed their propellor at the very head of the loch – since when they had been laboriously rowing in the direction of home. We took them in tow, and soon everyone was safely back, in need of a few drams but none the worse. Dinner started at 10. The venison was delicious, and the cook duly resigned, which was even better.

Consternation reigned again when Rory, one of the garrons, became bellied in a bog. The accident was in no way the fault of the pony, whose instinct for ground was unfailing; rather, it was due to wilful disregard of orders on the part of General Sir Richard Goodbody, a distinguished Gunner colleague of my father-in-law, who had nobly agreed to augment his regular duties in charge of the boiler-room by acting as pony-boy for the day, but then ignored his instructions, which were, whatever he did, not to take the pony off the path. When he saw a column of smoke beckoning from the hill with the news that a stag had been shot, instead of following the track, he made straight for the signal – and almost at once Rory sank up to his belly in a morass.

Luckily he had not gone far from the road or from the lodge, and by bringing out shed-doors and laying them in front of him, one after the other, rescuers were able to drag him out. All the same, he struggled so violently to extricate himself that blood began to pour from his mouth, and it looked as though he had sustained some severe internal rupture. John Lawrence (later Lord Oaksey), the well-known amateur jockey, advocated covering him with wet blankets, to slow down his circulation, and in due course he began shivering with cold. Huge relief greeted the late-night arrival of a vet, who found that the pony had only bitten its uvula, which would heal without treatment.

I happened to hear about one curious happening which had occurred at Loch Choire, not during any of our visits, but earlier, in the 1950s, when the sporting artist Raoul Millais often stalked on the forest as the guest of Geordie, the fifth Duke of Sutherland. Raoul – grandson of the pre-Raphaelite painter Sir John Everett Millais – was another gifted artist, who painted racehorses and hunters to great acclaim, and later turned to bull-fighting as a subject; but he also produced many evocative studies of the Scottish Highlands and the deer, which captured the light and space of the hills with soaring imagination.

Out one day with an old stalker called Duncan at the southern end of the forest, he came upon a stag with a broken front leg which limped away downhill towards a wood on the side of what he called the Black Loch, a thousand feet below them on their left. At once he became determined to finish the wounded beast off, and suggested that they should follow it; but Duncan absolutely refused to accompany him, saying that the wood was 'an awful queer place', into which wounded stags always disappeared, and that nothing would make him enter it.

Undeterred, Raoul hurtled down the steep face, sliding on patches of scree until he came to the edge of the wood, only to find that it was a ruin, in which hundreds of dead birches lay interlaced on the ground or were propped against a few living trees. Even as he began forcing his way into the tangle, still hoping to catch up with the wounded beast, he felt there was something eerie about the place, but he pressed on until he emerged into a more open glade.

He had taken only a few further steps when he heard a stick crack. He stopped. All around him ancient-looking stags – perhaps ten of them – were rising slowly to their feet. They were so dreadfully emaciated that when he mastered his astonishment he decided he must finish off as many as he could. He therefore shot three, before the rest – not reacting with anything like the speed of healthy animals – drifted slowly away into the gloom of the surrounding thickets. His most unnerving moment came when he went up to the nearest body and found he could lift it with one hand: it was no more than a bag of bones covered with skin like hairy parchment. Hastening to leave that sinister graveyard, he went on along the shore of the loch and found Duncan waiting for him by the boat.

'Ye look as if ye've seen a ghost, man,' said the stalker.

'I have,' Raoul told him. 'I've seen ten.'

Raoul was ninety-four when he told me this story. Knowing Loch Choire so well, I was fascinated by it, and tried to pin down precisely where the incident had occurred; but I could not match his description to features on the ground, even though he and I together pored over the one-inch Ordnance Survey map of the area. What he called the Black Loch can only have been the water officially known as Loch a' Bheallaich, unofficially the Top Loch; but there is no substantial area of woodland beside it, nor indeed space for one between the bottom of the steep face and the shore. I do not for a moment doubt the veracity of his account: as an artist, he had acute powers of observation, and he was an experienced stalker. Whatever he saw that day had haunted him for forty years – but it remains one of the unsolved mysteries of the hill.

5

A Look at the Past

T HE REALITY WAS THAT almost all my contacts with deer lay in
the south. Even though we went to Scotland almost every
autumn, it was only for a fortnight at most, and for the rest of the year
my stalking was in the woods near home. Nevertheless, the Highlands
had taken such a grip on my imagination that I began trying to spend
more time in the hills vicariously, by writing about them.

My first attempt was a novel, *The Megacull*, a thriller about a group
of Fascist fanatics who decide that the population of the United
Kingdom is far too large, and set about halving it by poisoning reser-
voirs of drinking water out in the mountains. The dastardly scheme
is discovered by the young narrator, who is stalking on an estate not
a million miles from Loch Choire, and detects sinister operations
brewing on the forest across the march. I never managed to make
details of the plot very convincing, but at least I was able to use the
background to which I had taken such a fancy – and the book found a
publisher, went into a second edition and came out in paperback.

Every time we went north, I became more curious about how the deer forests had been created, and I began to amass information about them by reading around the subject, with the aim of writing an account of how the Victorians and Edwardians had transformed millions of acres into a vast deer ranch. My research had perforce to be sporadic, since I had a full-time job in Fleet Street, and my quest spread out over several years; but it took me to places which I otherwise would probably never have seen. One was Balmoral, and another Blair Castle, home of the Duke of Atholl.

At Balmoral – which I visited through the kind auspices of the Resident Factor, Colonel William McHardy (and also, I presume, with the permission of Her Majesty the Queen), I was let loose in the library for a couple of days to study books of deer-stalking history which I could find nowhere else. It was a strange but profitable experience to be alone in the castle in mid-winter, surrounded by tartan and hellishly cold – and then the Colonel increased my debt to him by taking me on a tour of the estate.

Of special interest to me was an experiment organised by the Duke of Edinburgh, who had arranged for a small area of the ancient Ballochbuie pine forest to be fenced off so that the deer had no access to it. Outside the enclosed area, there were only mature Caledonian pines – lovely trees, with their pink bark and heavy canopy, perhaps three hundred years old. All the other vegetation had been eaten down to within an inch or less of the ground, and not a single young tree was growing. But, with the deer excluded, the natural regeneration inside the trial plot was astonishing. Scots pine seedlings had sprung up by the hundred, several to every square yard, and between them birch, heather, blaeberry and other shrubs had began to establish a dense understorey, offering an idea of how rich the Caledonian forest of antiquity must have been.

At Blair, Ian, Duke of Atholl, gave me an equally clear run in the castle's fascinating Charter Room. Estate records furnished some idea of how his ancestors had organised the Tinchels – the ancient form of hunting in which perhaps a thousand men, accompanied by as many dogs as they could muster, went off into the hills and formed an immense cordon, staying out for a week or more, carrying their food and sleeping wrapped in their plaids. Face by face, ridge by ridge, corrie by corrie they drove the deer inwards towards a narrow pass or between stone walls which gradually converged into a long, narrowing funnel. This led to a circular enclosure known as an elrig, in which the trapped deer could be slaughtered with bows and arrows, pikes, broadswords and daggers. At the great hunt held on Atholl ground in 1563, for the entertainment of Mary Queen of Scots, many of the deer escaped, but three hundred and sixty were killed, along with five wolves.

As I plodded up the bare hills at Loch Choire, I was fascinated by the ancient tree-roots, white with age, which protruded from the sides of peat hags. How old were they, and why had the trees died out?

It seems that in about 9000 BC, when the last Ice Age was ending, and the glaciers which had covered Scotland were pulling back towards the north at a rate of about six miles in every century, trees began to establish themselves in the mineral-rich earth exposed by the melting ice. Analysis of pollen suggests that wind-borne seeds started to grow no more than three hundred yards from the retreating ice walls, and gradually a huge forest spread across the mountains, reaching a height of 2000 feet in the west and 3000 feet in the east. The trees were never densely massed, as in the dark, serried ranks of latter-day plantations: rather, Scots pine, oak, birch, alder and hazel of all ages were loosely scattered, with good grazing among them and shelter for animals. In that grand Caledonian forest lived brown bears, wild oxen, wild boar, wolves, lynx, beavers and roe deer – and red deer half as big again as those of today. I like to think that the forest also contained that amazing creature, the Gigantic Irish Elk – a grotesque-looking monster with antlers ten or twelve feet wide, which went extinct at the onset of the last Ice Age, some twelve thousand years ago.

Over the millennia the forest cover gradually disappeared – and humans were responsible for at least some of its destruction. Sometimes they set fire to whole stretches of woodland, to flush out enemies. They felled thousands of trees to clear land for agriculture and to furnish building materials for houses and ships, and later they cut down thousands more to feed furnaces for smelting iron. But I suspect that these activities had far less effect than the violent swings of climate which turned the weather from relatively mild and dry to cold and wet, led to the formation of enormous deposits of peat, and impoverished much of the land so severely that no useful plants or trees would grow on it. As a result, the red deer were obliged to expend a great deal of their energy on merely maintaining their body temperature, and consequently became much diminished in stature.

Until well into the eighteenth century the owners of great Scottish estates rarely went out stalking. Such activity was deemed neither dignified nor customary: rather, it was left to one of the forest staff, whose duty it was to supply house or castle with venison. Then, gradually, the lairds began to pursue the deer themselves: in 1732 Lord George Murray, younger brother of the second Duke of Atholl, spent the whole summer hunting in Glen Tatinich, and in frequent letters to his wife described how he was enjoying 'the most noble Divertion in the world,' and how the exercise had put him 'in perfect health, & indeed I never was better.'

Later, in the eighteenth and nineteenth centuries, more members of the Atholl family and their friends also developed a taste for individual stalking. Other lairds followed their example; but it was not until the 1830s that English sportsmen started to head for the Highlands in any numbers. Foremost among the pioneers was William Scrope, author of *The Art of Deer-Stalking*, first published in 1838, and a collector's item to this day. A landed gentlemen, with property in several counties, and a friend of the novelist Sir Walter Scott, Scrope took Glen Bruar from the Duke of Atholl year after year, and stalked the ground with boundless enthusiasm. His book (in my view) is spoilt by its excessively facetious tone, but his narrative includes many splendid chases, triumphs and disasters; and the battered woodwork of his seven rifles, displayed in the castle at Blair Atholl, gives a vivid

idea of the difficulties of using muzzle-loaders, which he usually flung
to the ground after a shot so that he could grab a second weapon from
his ghillie and have another chance. As he himself remarked, 'rock or
moss, it [the rifle] took its chance'.

When I read about the formation of the deer forests, I found that
many authors blamed the Victorians for the notorious Highland
Clearances, in which thousands of people were evicted from their
homes in the glens and forced to seek refuge in the slums of Scottish
cities, or to emigrate to America, Canada and Australia. That
appalling cruelties were perpetrated, there is no doubt. Whole settle-
ments of hovels were set on fire without warning. The inhabitants
were left homeless and lost all their possessions. Many died of exposure or disease. Moreover, the communities in Sutherland – the only
area of which I had any experience so far – were among the worst-
afflicted, and in 1815 Patrick Sellar, factor to Elizabeth Countess of
Sutherland and her husband the Marquess of Stafford, was arrested on
charges of wilful cruelty. At his trial he was exonerated, but to this day
his name is execrated in the far north.

Yet the Clearances began in the late eighteenth century and continued early in the nineteenth, before the vogue for Highland sport
took hold, and they were carried out on the orders of avaricious
lairds who thought they could make more money from Cheviot sheep
than they could extort in rent from impoverished humans. Between
about 1780 and 1830 sheep walks, or ranches, were created all over
Scotland; but according to the second Earl of Malmesbury, who
became an authority on the subject, it was only in 1833 that the Highlands 'became the rage' among sportsmen.

Before that, a few intrepid English shooting men had made expeditions into the far north, and, as Malmsesbury recorded, 'a stranger
could fish and shoot over almost any part of the Highlands without
interruption, the letting value of the *ferae naturae* being unknown to
their possessors.' The Earl himself stalked at Achnacarry, the great
estate belonging to Cameron of Lochiel, which had been a deer forest

for generations. But from 1840 or so southerners began to create new sporting estates of their own by renting or buying huge tracts of land which they 'afforested', or set aside, purely for stalking, fishing and grouse-shooting. They spent fortunes not only on the land itself, but also on building lodges equipped with deer-larders and kennels, roads to open up their new properties, bridges over burns and rivers, and pony paths so that remote areas could be reached and deer could be more easily brought off the hill.

In researching the subject, I had one great stroke of luck, when Freddie Wills, then part-owner with his brother Tom of Coulin, in Wester Ross, lent me a box of papers relating to the creation of the forest. Here, in the original documents, was a blow-by-blow account of how in 1866 the fifteenth Lord Elphinstone bought 16,000 acres of mountain land for £40,000 and created a sporting estate out of the wilderness. One of his first acts was to clear his ground of sheep, so as to improve the grazing for the deer, and before he could build a new lodge, he had to put in a road to the site he had chosen. Luckily he had an agreeable neighbour in the form of Sir Kenneth Mackenzie, proprietor of the adjoining Kinlochewe. When Elphinstone wrote asking permission to put in the road across part of his land, Mackenzie replied:

I don't the least want to see the plan of your road, so you are very welcome to set to work on it whenever you like. The only thing I would suggest is that you should *bridge* at a place or in a manner that will not interfere with the fishing.

The road cost £568 3s 11½d, and two bridges £460. The timber for these came from more than forty large pines, felled locally. The lodge itself – a relatively modest building, but incorporating a chapel for the spiritual welfare of the family and its retainers – cost just over £5000, together with nearly £500 for the furnishings. A water supply was arranged by tapping one of the burns, and pony-paths were laid out by hand at a cost of 'one penny per lineal yard four feet wide with side drains where necessary'. Almost all the expenditure went to masons, carpenters, general labourers and carters living in the immediate vicinity, so that the local economy benefited greatly from the project. Elphinstone's total outlay amounted to £8002, and once the lodge was inhabited, his family, guests and servants created a strong demand for groceries, beer, whisky and other domestic necessities, not least bottles of King of Oudh's Sauce.

This process, repeated all over the Highlands, gradually transformed several million acres into a gigantic deer ranch. Some of the new lairds were content to leave their marches open and unmarked, delineated only by lines drawn on maps; but others insisted on building mile upon mile of fences – and on high, rocky ground the construction of these barriers was a formidable task, for the workmen had to carry out all their materials, drill holes in rock, and set every metal post in molten lead. Most of the fences were only three or four feet high, and although they would contain sheep, they presented no obstacle to the deer, which could easily jump over them. Today most of the barriers have collapsed, but thousands of posts remain in situ, and lengths of rusty wire lie twisting about among the rocks – reminders of the immense efforts that were made 150 years ago.

No matter how well the new estate roads were laid down, travel along their gravel surfaces in jolting horse-drawn carriages was thoroughly uncomfortable, and if a lodge stood on or near the shore of a loch, a more agreeable way to approach it was by boat. When Walter Shoolbred, proprietor of a high-class joinery firm, wanted to put up a house at the western end of Loch Glass, in his newly acquired forest of Wyvis, in Ross-shire, he first built a steam yacht and launched it at the eastern end of the water, so that all his construction materials could be carried easily to the site. When the lodge was finished, he and his guests travelled comfortably, admiring the scenery, for the last few miles of their journey.

Another much-used vessel was the *Rifle*, an iron steam yacht built in about 1861, which plied up and down Loch Arkaig for years, acting as general transport for everyone on the Achnacarry Estate: a

Victorian photograph shows it alongside a pier, with a woman and baby on board, a sheep-dog on the stern, and altogether about twenty-five people either embarking or disembarking.* In wild and difficult country steam yachts became fashionable. When Sir John Stirling-Maxwell built his lodge at Corrour, near Fort William in the 1890s, he installed a yacht, the *Cailleach*, on Loch Ossian so that visitors were saved a three-mile road journey and could proceed smoothly to the pier right in front of the house.

This great surge in afforestation was disastrous for the environment. With the humans (who used to poach all year round) swept out of the glens, and with most of the sheep (which no longer paid) got rid of, the deer increased enormously. Some were culled every year, of course, but most of the new lairds exercised restraint, so that the herds steadily built up – and the result was ruinous. Being browsers as well as grazers – that is, eating leaves and the shoots of trees and shrubs, as well as grass – the deer combined with the remaining sheep to destroy most of the forest that remained, and so condemned themselves to a life on the open hill.

Reminders of the past haunt every Highland glen, and no latter-day stalker can fail to be moved by the evidence of earlier human habitation. Look down from the heights as you pursue the deer, and by the side of burn or loch far below you will see tiny squares and rectangles marked out by the stumps of walls – the outlines of primitive houses. A stone chimney, still standing, commemorates the site of a modest dwelling. Bigger patches of green encircled by broken-down walls are all that remain of the sheilings in which people gathered their black cattle long ago. Short, parallel ridges like those on a draining board, still visible in the grass or heather, are the only sign of the lazy-beds in which they grew potatoes and other vegetables. There, a thousand feet below you lies the ghost of a settlement, which will never come back to life.

* The yacht eventually sank in the loch, but part of it was brought to the surface in 2001, and is now in the Scottish Maritime Museum in Irvine.

My history of the deer forests, *Monarchs of the Glen*, came out in 1978, and some time after its publication I was invited to lunch at Achnacarry Castle by Donald Cameron of Lochiel, the fourteenth member of the family to bear that title. A man of perfect natural courtesy, he said he had enyoyed the book, but in the most gentle-manly fashion he suggested that I might have benefited in my re-search by asking to look through the records of his forest. I knew that he was right – for after a great deal of searching elsewhere, I had run out of time and energy, and had failed to approach him. I much regretted this, and still do, for many stirring events had occurred at Achnacarry – not least the death of the young Earl of Dalkeith on 17 September 1886.

The stalking party travelled up Loch Arkaig on the *Rifle*, went ashore on the south side and set off on a long, hard climb up the hill called Gulvain, armed with a .450 double-barrelled Express. Late in the afternoon they came within range of three stags, and John Cameron, the Head Stalker, told Dalkeith to fire at one of them. At the shot the stag bolted, but clearly it had been hit, and after quickly re-loading Dalkeith ran forward, only to slip on wet grass and tumble headlong down a steeply sloping rock slab. Cameron shouted at him to throw the rifle away, but before he could do so, it went off, wounding him fatally. The bullet shattered his left shoulder and ruptured the axillary artery in his chest. His companions were unable to staunch the internal bleeding, and in little more than an hour he was dead.

A ghillie was despatched to tell the captain of the *Rifle* to steam back to the castle and bring help; but by then darkness had fallen, and the hill was so steep and dangerous that Cameron and the second ghillie did not dare to start taking the body down until the moon rose at 3 am. Then, having wrapped it in their plaids, they managed to bring it to the lochside, where they were met by a team of estate men and the local doctor.

A century later I myself went out on Gulvain with Alistair Morris, a large and cheerful young stalker, and as we looked down on the dark water of Loch Arkaig I kept thinking of Dalkeith's wretched end. Our luck was better than his, for we got an eighteen-stone stag which had been causing havoc in one of the plantations; but then, in 1990, fate struck again, and Alistair was killed in a freak accident on the road, when an oncoming timber lorry shed its load on a bend, and logs smashed through the windscreen of his car.

6

Mistakes

AUTUMN AFTER AUTUMN we returned to Loch Choire. In time
McNichol retired, and was succeeded by Jock Cairney, then in
his thirties – lean, dark-bearded, not given to suffering fools, but an
excellent stalker and hill-man. He was also a wizard at catching
salmon, and if ever we wanted one for the table, he would go off
down the river (after a ritual discharge of obscenities), and return in a
remarkably short time with a couple of fine fish. Colin also retired,
and was replaced by Willie Clark, a small man with a lugubrious
expression, a great imbiber with the reputation of having been been
a leading poacher, who went to the hill wearing Wellington boots on
his out-turned feet. Willie claimed to be a 'verra puir short' with a
shotgun, but he enjoyed relating his one big triumph, years ago, when
he potted a heron as it laboured up the Helmsdale. 'I was there, in the
barnk,' he would say, eyes shining. 'I waited till he was right in front
of me, and then BARNG! Boy! There was nothing but a cloud of
feathers!'

His best narrative, though, concerned an occasion on which he had been acting as stalker to a certain lord:

'Crawl in. Party of five stags, starnding nicely.

'"Take the blarck one on the left, M'Lord".

'BARNG! Mussed! "Fire again, M' Lord."

'BARNG! Mussed! "Ye're over, M' Lord. Fire again."

'BARNG! Mussed! The stags run a bit. They're confused – don't know where the shots are coming from.

'Doun! Barck! Come up on a rock, and Christ – here's the stags, stell starnding. "Fire, M'Lord." BARNG! Mussed!

'"That's it, M'Lord. Awa' home."'

That noble rifleman was by no means the only person to make a fool of himself. One Sunday, with no shooting or stalking in prospect, I decided to go for a solitary hike. Perhaps I was over-confident, perhaps merely careless; but the fact was that I made a series of mistakes which caused my family dreadful anxiety and ruined what should have been an agreeable evening. First, I failed to tell anyone exactly what I was proposing to do; second, I did not arm myself with a compass; third, I did not take any food with me. I did not need to carry water, for there were burns everywhere on the hill.

My plan was simple: I intended merely to walk out to the bhealaich – the pass beyond the Top Loch – and then swing in a left-handed semi-circle across the high ground before dropping back down to the side of Loch Choire itself, and returning along the shore to the lodge. Had things gone right, I would probably have walked about twelve or fifteen miles, but I reckoned that that was well within my capabilities, and that I had plenty of time to cover the distance.

To start off, I hitched a lift with a party going up Loch Choire by boat for a picnic on the beach at the far end. From there I set off up the path beside the Top Loch at about 1 pm. The day was cool and grey, with heavy cloud-cover – ideal for walking – and at the start all went well. I was wearing a new pair of the special hill shoes made by Hogg of Fife, heavily nailed and with up-turned toes which made the owner look a bit like Mickey Mouse, but were supposed

to facilitate progress uphill. Although the studs grated on rock –
a hazard if I had been stalking – the shoes gripped well and felt
comfortable.

When I climbed to the pass, I found that the wind was blowing
straight in my face, from the south-west. Leaving the path, I turned
ninety degrees to my left and climbed to my first objective, the Sandy
Loch – a sheet of ruffled grey water lying in a high cradle of rocks. A
pair of mergansers went off it as I appeared, skimming away low over
the surface, and a lone cock grouse got up under my feet, which I took
as a sign of good luck. Then I set out across a desolate wildness which
I had never seen before.

The land up there, at 1200 or 1500 feet, was quite different from the
much fiercer ground on the Klibreck side of the forest. Instead of
steep, rocky faces, there were long, gently undulating sweeps of fea-
tureless, dun-coloured moorland, which the stalkers called 'the flows',
each one sinking in the middle and rising again to a small, rounded
ridge or hill-top, with nothing to identify one from another. Here and
there black peat hags with walls three or four feet high held pools of
water, but they were easily circumvented, and the going was quite
easy. For the time being I was not worried by the lack of distinguish-
ing features. All I had to do (I thought) was to hold the wind steady on
my right cheek and keep walking.

In retrospect, it seems astonishing that I went on for so long before
anxiety began to bite. Even when the clouds closed down, and wraiths
of mist began to drift across the hill, I was not worried. I just kept
going, with the occasional pause to watch a herd of deer through
binoculars. After a while I began to think that I must be fairly close
above Loch Choire, below me on the left, and that when I reached the
next little ridge or summit, I would find myself looking down on the
familiar, long strip of water.

Somehow that did not happen. When I came up to the next crest,
beyond it lay not the loch, but another sweep of anonymous moorland, exactly the same as the one I had just crossed, dipping in the
middle and rising to yet another crest. Stepping up my pace, I reached

the next ridge with the same expectation – and the same disappointment greeted me.

The mist was thickening, and the light was beginning to fade. I sat
down on a rock and stared at my map, struggling to work out where
I was. The wind was still on my right cheek, and I thought I had been
holding a good course; but somehow I conceived the notion that I had
gone too far to my left, and that I should aim more to the right. After
the event, it became perfectly obvious that this idea was ridiculous –
for if I *had* gone too far to the left, in too tight a semi-circle, I would
have come out above the loch hours earlier. Nevertheless, defying
logic, my brain told me to head right-handed, and so I did.

Somewhere in front of me, I felt sure, striking across my line of
advance, was the pony path that ran for four miles up from the lodge
and over the top to the Shellachan stable in its fold beside a burn. I
started to think of this path as a kind of safety net: once I hit it, all I
would have to do would be to turn left and follow it home.

I set off again. I was growing tired, and by that stage my new shoes
had chewed the backs of my heels into blisters, which were smarting
uncomfortably, but my only option was to ignore the pain and carry
on. Then at last came a surge of relief: as I cleared yet another ridge
and looked down, there below me stood a little wooden building,
its planks grey with age. The stable! 'Thank God,' I thought. 'I can
manage now.'

And yet, as I went down to it, alarm came needling in. I had seen
the Shellachan stable only once, and could not remember it precisely;
but somehow neither this building nor its situation seemed right. The
structure itself was the wrong shape, and there was no burn close to
it. Even worse, there was no well-used track running past it. For a
minute or two I tried to persuade myself that this *was* the Shellachan
stable: that I had remembered the details wrong, or was looking at
the building from a different angle. But wishful thinking could not
disguise the reality for long: this was some remote bothy which I
had never visited before. I was utterly lost, and dusk was coming
on. Scrutiny of the map produced no answer to my problems: no

building was marked anywhere near where I thought I was. My only hope was to keep walking across the wretched, interminable flows.

Still I was nursing the same certainty – that when I reached the next ridge, I *must* see down on the loch. Imagine the shock, when I came to the umpteenth crest, looked over, and saw not a sheet of water, but, plummeting away below me, a deep, steep-sided glen with a river flowing through it and a house on the far bank. A house! I knew for sure that there were no outlying houses on Loch Choire forest. This, then, must be an abandoned croft.

Night was coming on. All round me dusk was sliding into the hollows, filling them with pools of darkness. I sat down on a rock and made one final attempt to read the map. But by then the light was so poor, and I was so tired, that my brain simply could not work out what had gone wrong. Nor had I any idea of what to do. I felt stunned and helpless. It was already well past eight o'clock, and everyone at the lodge must be wondering where I was, yet I had no means of communicating with them.

I hauled myself to my feet, only to see that down in the supposedly derelict croft a light had gone on. So the place was inhabited! Clearly, I must go down to it. Instantly I charged off down the dangerously steep face, risking a broken leg or ankle as I plunged recklessly between rocks and then, lower down, through bracken. At the bottom I found that the river was flowing fast from left to right but I waded straight across, thigh-deep, and went up to the front door of the house.

I knocked, and a moment later it opened. A man stood outlined against the light.

'Sorry to bother you,' I began, 'but I'm lost.'

'Where are ye from?'

'Loch Choire. Where's this?'

'Christ, man! Ye're at Ben Armine.'

Ben Armine! I was miles from base. The man's name, I discovered, was Eric McLeod. Seeing how exhausted I was, he said, 'Ye'd better come in and sit down. Ye're wet through, as well.' I realised from his voice and clothes that he must be the local stalker. In the warm kitchen his wife immediately began offering me food and tea. I was too tired to eat anything, but cup after cup of heavily-sugared tea brought me to my senses and stepped up my anxiety about the nuisance I must be causing at Loch Choire, because Ben Armine then had no means of communication with the outside world.

Presently Eric said, 'I'll need to drive you back.' Noble as the offer was, I could not take it up. By pony path, the distance to home was only nine miles, but by road the lodge was ninety miles away, twenty of them along execrable gravel tracks. The journey would take over three hours in a Land Rover. Already it was past 9 pm. If Eric did give me a lift, he would have a seven-hour drive, and would not be home until four in the morning. I could not possibly impose on him to such an extent. Instead, I announced that I would walk. A good pony path, I knew, followed the burn the whole way up to the Shellachan stable, and from there led directly on home.

My kind hosts did their best to dissuade me, offering a bed for the night, but I had become obsessed by the need to let my own people know what was happening, and at about 9.30 I set off uphill into the dark, carrying a paper bag of sandwiches which Eric's wife had pressed upon me. As I left, his last words came after me: 'Whatever ye do, don't leave the path.'

Ironically – now that it no longer had the power to disorientate me – the mist had lifted. The sky was still covered with clouds, but some moonlight was filtering through them, and the night was not particularly dark. I could easily pick out the line of the path stretching up the hill ahead of me, and avoid holes in the track. The burn kept me noisy company, tumbling over rocks in its channel on my left, and soon I threw my sandwiches into it, thinking that the trout might as well have them.

The first hour passed without causing me much distress: rejuvenated by the intake of tea and sugar, I strode out as fast as I could, ignoring the pain in my heels and wondering all the time what members of my family were doing. I feared that they had gone out into the mountains in search of me, and would themselves get lost or injured.

Increasing exhaustion gradually slowed my pace. Every step began to seem an effort, and I cast covetous glances at the little bridges of smooth wooden planks which carried the path over tributary burns. The idea of lying down on one of them for a rest became irresistibly seductive. I knew I should resist the temptation, because to fall asleep would be dangerous. The night air had turned cold, and if hypothermia set in, I might never wake up. All the same ... just a few minutes would surely do no harm.

At the next bridge, I tramped over the boards and carried on; but at the one beyond it I gave in and lay down flat on my back. The relief was glorious. I was hot from the exertion of walking uphill, and the wooden slats seemed as soft as a feather bed... but I must have gone straight to sleep and remained unconscious quite a while, for when I came round I was shuddering with cold. Aching all over, but scared back into full wakefulness, I struggled to my feet and carried on.

At last, around 11 pm, I reached the Shellachan stable. The moment I saw the place, I rejoiced. This really *was* the building I had visited once before. Even in the dark I recognised its shape, and its snug setting beside the burn. Here, close by it, was the junction of the paths, where the track I had been following went straight on, and the one that I needed branched off to the left. Once on that, I had four miles to go, and no fear of making any more mistakes.

Four miles! After what I had already been through, the prospect was appalling. Yet I had no choice but to stumble on. In a few more minutes I realised I had crossed the watershed, and the ground was beginning to fall. Then suddenly, down in the darkness ahead of me, I saw two little spurts of fire. A moment later I heard a faint *pop-pop*. Somebody was out looking for me, trying to attract my attention by firing both barrels of a shotgun. I shouted as loud as I could, but the sound was lost in the vast expanses of the hill. All I could do was hurry on forward. Soon two more little flashes sparked into the night, brighter this time, and the double shots sounded louder. Again

I yelled, but again there was no response. Only after the third little volley did I get an answer. Seconds later a blundering rush brought me face to face with a man standing on the path. By his stance and dimly seen beard I recognised him as Jock Cairney, our head stalker.

'Devil 'a God, man,' he cried. 'Where've you been?'

I started to blurt out something about getting lost, but he turned on his heel without another word and set off down the hill at a fearful pace, leaving me to stagger after him as best I could. By the time we reached the lodge, soon after midnight, I was all in. I was too exhausted to eat, and my heels had been chewed into ribbons – and of course I was deservedly met with recrimination from all directions. Everyone had been out looking for me, supposing that I had fallen, broken a leg and was lying out on the hill, or, at best, crawling towards home. I do not remember exactly what happened, but I think I was told to have a hot bath and go to bed. In the morning I learnt that my father-in-law had disappeared into the night on a search of his own, and had not regained the lodge until 4 am, having gone for a marathon trek round the mountain; but then, being an essentially cheerful person, he had decided to celebrate my return by having a bath in the Duke's colossal tub, with a bottle of champagne at his elbow.

Trying to analyse what had gone wrong, I came to the conclusion that during the afternoon the wind must have swung round from south-west to north-west, so that although I kept it on my right cheek, it was sending me away from home, in quite the wrong direction. But I could never explain the mystery of why my brain had persistently told me to aim further to the right. Somebody suggested it was because one of my legs was longer than the other – an idea I did not find convincing. All I knew for sure was that I had made an idiot of myself, and had been lucky to get away with it.

A far worse setback occurred on a brilliantly fine day at the end of September 1964, when a party went walking-up grouse along the precipitous southern flank of Klibreck. The left-hand gun, lowest in the line, was Nick Yeatman-Biggs, who found himself hurrying to keep up with the rest. As he went to cross the lip of a waterfall where the Black Burn emerged from its corrie and ran out over a steep drop, he lost his foothold. A second later he was falling, bouncing off rocks. As he dropped, he threw away his shotgun, which went off when it landed, but he himself hurtled on down, mainly on his backside, until he crashed into a shallow pool some 150 feet below. He managed to crawl to the edge of the water, but when he looked over, he found that there was another vertical drop straight below, so he dragged himself out at the side of the pool and lay on a rock. When he tried to get to his feet, he found he could not stand.

It was lunch time, and by pre-arrangement the other members of the party had started closing up to the middle of the line to sit down and eat their pieces. The face of the hill was so rough – all rocky out-crops, little cliffs and hollows – that nobody had witnessed Nick's fall; but one of them, Jane Mills, had a hunch that something bad had hap-pened, and twice forced the others to initiate searches. The first sweep drew blank, but Jane insisted that they try again, and a second hunt some time later at last revealed a hand waving feebly from below.

My brother-in-law Gerry Barstow, who was in the territorial SAS, immediately launched a rescue operation – no easy task, as the acci-dent had occurred high up the hill five miles from base. Nick was wet through, shocked, and in severe pain. While the rest of the party wrapped him in their jackets and began lowering him down the face towards the loch-side, Gerry and a colleague ran for the boats left at the top of the big loch. Two of the wives – Susannah Yeatman-Biggs (Nick's wife) and Sue Mills (sister-in-law of Jane), both heavily preg-nant – had been pottering along the shore, and were startled to see the men running towards them.

Taking both outboard motors for security – and one did break down on the way – all four of them motored to the lodge, where they improvised a stretcher from the frame of a bed, lashing oars across the top and car tyres to the underside to give it some primitive cushioning. As they worked, someone took off in a car for Kinbrace to telephone for an ambulance (the radio link having closed down for the day).

Back at the head of the loch, the rescuers loaded the casualty on to the stretcher, laid it across the gunwales of the boat and set off for home as gently as they could. By the time they were back at the lodge, dark had fallen. Susannah and Sue Mills followed the ambulance out along the eleven miles of private road, wincing every time they saw the vehicle bobble over a stone or lurch into a pothole – and the driver (quite rightly) crawled along so slowly that it was midnight, nearly twelve hours after Nick had fallen, before they reached the hospital in Golspie.

There he spent the next month, wonderfully looked after by the doctors and nurses. It turned out that he had cracked his pelvis and several vertebrae, and was hideously bruised all down his back; but he did not need any operation, and he mended up so well that he was left, as he himself put it, 'only slightly lopsided'. His gun came off less well: its triggers and trigger-guard had been hammered flat against the bottom of the action by impact on a rock, and it was a write-off.

The worst feature of his stay in hospital was that local journalists got wind of the accident, probably through the police or the ambulance service, and rang up relentlessly, again and again, probing for details and insinuating that the whole affair – because it involved a gun – had been an attempt at suicide or murder. So persistent were they that, in order to frustrate them, Gerry (a solicitor) wrote a definitive account of what had happened.

As if not enough were going on at Loch Choire, we were often most hospitably entertained by Alba Paynter, widow of the distinguished soldier Sir George Paynter, who owned the Suisgill estate on the Helmsdale. Every now and then she would send up a message on the evening radio link saying, 'Can you spare two young men to walk-up grouse tomorrow?' The answer was invariably 'Yes!' – and enormous fun we had, for there were far more grouse at Suisgill, where the heather was properly managed, and the stalker-keeper, Donald, kept excellent pointers.

Not that the grouse were the only attraction. Lady Paynter was a most generous hostess, bringing delicious lunches to the hill in the panniers of a garron, and laying on monumental teas when we came in from shooting. The heavy furniture in her lodge always made me think that the setting would be ideal for a murder play by Agatha Christie, in which the butler would be found skewered to the under-side of the billiard table with a carving knife; but outside she had created a glorious garden – unique in that harsh environment – which astonished everyone who drove up the strath with its blaze of colour.

By the time we knew her, she was already of a certain age, and her favourite companion was a rangy apricot poodle called Waffle. This creature could do no wrong. In her eyes he was a brilliant retriever – and it was true that he would run-in like the wind after every shot, clearing the heather in flying bounds. It was also true that he would pick up a grouse. But he would then give the bird such a fearful bite as to send its innards flying backwards out of it, rendering it unfit for the table or for sale. To Donald, whose dogs were perfectly trained, Waffle was an insufferable menace, and in moments of extreme vex-ation he would mutter '*Shoot the f_ _ _ _ _ !*', followed by a long-drawn-out groan of 'Oh, buggering hell!'

The trouble, as he knew perfectly well, was that Waffle ruled the roost. One day, as we were walking in line for grouse, lunch time was approaching, and because I knew that our hostess would be coming up with the pony, I asked Donald if it was still safe to shoot in front. 'Aye,' he replied. 'I don't mind if you shoot her ladyship, but for Christ's sake don't shoot Waffle!' Hardly had he uttered these immor-tal words when, to my surprise, I spotted antlers sticking up out of a hollow down to my right. It seemed a very strange place to see a stag, and at first I supposed the animal must be dead. Then I saw the antlers move slightly, and I knew at once that something was wrong, because we had been firing shots not far off, and any sound beast would long since have departed.

Hurrying close, I found that the wretched animal had got entan-gled in fence wire, and in its struggles had laced its back legs to its head, so that its whole body was twisted round in a tight hoop. The moment it saw me, it made grotesque efforts to stand up, but all it achieved was to roll about, out of control, and I instantly decided that the best thing to do was to put it out of its misery, as its only other fate would be to die of thirst and starvation. Watching my moment, I darted in and fired the left barrel of my 12-bore into the back of its neck from a distance of about a foot. The shot knocked it unconscious long enough for me to stick it in the throat with my knife, and gradually its struggles ceased.

Donald approved of what I had done, even though he lamented the loss of a good stag, a seven-pointer about six years old, and weighing perhaps sixteen stone. As we had no means of moving it, and he did not want to disrupt the shoot, we left it where it lay. When Lady Paynter appeared with the lunch, swathed as usual in yards of plaid, we teased her a bit by saying that so far we had got one beast, but that as it was rather rubbishy, we would try for a better one in the afternoon. We kept her mystified for several minutes, and she took the ribbing in good part.

7

Hambleden

AFTER EVERY SOJOURN in the spaces of the far north, the Chilterns at first seemed rather tame; but as I became more professional, I began to cull deer on other estates, among them Hambleden, a magnificent, heavily wooded property of some 3000 acres which runs northwards into the hills from the river near Henley-on-Thames. No systematic control had ever been carried out there: the deer were running riot, and the order went out from the agent to shoot as many as possible.

Rising to the challenge, I bought a rifle of my own: a Holland & Holland .300 magnum, by no means new, but in excellent condition and fitted with a 4 x 32 telescopic sight set on a beautifully hand-made detachable mount. Carried away by the rifle's elegance and ease of handling, I did not at first realise that it was a much more powerful weapon than I needed, and would have despatched most species of big game. Being fairly large myself, I was not bothered by its recoil, but I soon found that it was liable to make a mess of a carcase if a shot was hurried or careless.

At first, I am afraid, my culling was not as selective as it might have been. The farmers, vociferous in their complaints, urged me to shoot what they called 'they bloody old stags' – and it was true that in summer and autumn senior fallow bucks did considerable damage to crops of wheat and barley. Wandering through them with their heads lowered, munching as they went, they knocked down more corn than they ate by flattening it with their antlers – and they made things even worse whenever they took up permanent residence in a crop, sleeping comfortably where they fed and laying still larger areas low.

Answering a typical summons one fine evening, I cautiously approached a field in which a dozen bucks had often been seen, and lay down in a hedge, covering the point at which they were most likely to emerge, with my head out one side and my feet out the other. With the air still and the sun setting behind me, the scene was so peaceful that I found it hard to stay awake. But then, after about half an hour, I suddenly felt something grab the heel of my right boot, and looking round I saw it was fast in the jaws of an Alsatian. Close behind the dog came the farmer, and when I whispered, 'Just waiting to see if they'll come out,' he roared, 'OH, ARRRH! GOOD OIDEER' in a voice that must have carried into the next county, thereby putting paid to that evening's operation.

I shot a considerable number of bucks without much discrimination, not yet realising that the only way to achieve a significant reduction in any deer population is to concentrate on culling females. Fallow does almost infallibly give birth to a fawn every year, but during the rut one buck will cover twenty or thirty does if he gets the chance, so that eliminating him merely gives some rival the chance to take over. Shooting selected bucks does achieve some measure of quality control, but not of quantity.

Whenever presented with a choice, I did try to take out animals with bad antlers or obvious signs of injury, and I began to build up a collection of deformed heads which I could use for demonstration purposes at talks to local societies. A curious fact is that an injury – to a leg or a testicle – often produces a deformity on the opposite side of the body: a broken right back leg, for instance, may well lead, in the following year, to the buck growing no antler on the left. Another characteristic of deer is that they have astonishing powers of recovery: I have often culled healthy beasts lacking the bottom joint of one leg (probably snapped by entanglement in a fence), or with a leg that has been broken in some collision and has knitted up crooked but perfectly strong.

Over the years I assembled a collection of freak antlers, and occasionally, when giving a talk to some local branch of the British Deer Society, I would use them to demonstrate various points. People usually showed quite keen interest; but one summer's evening, when I had a dozen visitors sitting on the lawn at home, I noticed that they were growing rather restive, and for a minute or two I feared I was becoming even more boring than usual. Then a noise made me look round, and I realised that right behind me a swarm of bees was condensing at high speed into the tight formation which they adopt in the last few seconds before descending on to the branch of a tree or some other handy support. It looked very much as if they had selected my head as their preferred landing-ground, and a rapid evacuation of the garden ensued. Only when the swarm had settled safely on to a gatepost could we resume our discussion.

Of the freak heads I amassed, the most striking was from a buck with a pair of short, perfectly straight antlers, lacking forks or points – just two spikes about a foot long spread in a V formation. When I saw that peculiar head through binoculars, as the light was coming up one morning, I at first thought the animal was a pricket; but soon I realised that it was an old beast with an enormous body, and that something must be wrong to have made it grow a head like that. I therefore shot it, and in the larder the mystery was solved. All over its skull were lead pellets, embedded under the skin. Somebody had peppered it with a shotgun during early summer, when its new antlers were growing, and although its eyes had miraculously escaped injury, the pellets had impeded the supply of blood to the coronets and stopped normal development. Instead of going into the antlers, the growth had gone onto the body: the buck was immensely stout, with a layer of fat three or four inches thick all along its back, and it weighed 200 lbs. The head (which I still have) provided a perfect illustration of the iniquities of using shotguns on deer.

Many indelible memories linger from crystalline winter mornings on those rolling, wooded hills. Once, as I looked out through a gap in a hedge, I found mist spread over a field in a low blanket. Normally fog makes stalking impossible; but this mist was so low, and lying in such a clearly defined layer, only about two feet thick, that I could see a buck feeding out in the middle of it. Its legs were hidden, but its head and the top half of its body were in sight. Whenever it started to graze, its head vanished, and I realised that it was in effect blindfolded. To make myself invisible was child's play: I simply went down on hands and knees and began crawling. It was cold work, as there was ice in every little depression, but the wind was in my favour, and I made good progress, raising my head every now and then to check that the buck was still there. Then, just as I judged I was within range, I surfaced to have another look – and by God, my target had disappeared. What spooked it, I never knew: like the Snark, it had softly and silently vanished away, and I was left covered in mud, with frozen knees and hands.

All woodland deer have a knack of disappearing suddenly: they melt into their surroundings like wraiths, screened by leaves and tree trunks, becoming part of the forest, and once they have been shifted, they are hard to find again. Early one August morning I moved out of a stand of superannuated hazel and began to walk slowly across the bottom of a small, rough field which rose steeply on my left, covered in rank weeds. After I had gone a few paces something made me look up the hill, and there, no more than twenty yards away, screened by a mass of head-high thistledown, was the shape of a deer. So thick was the thistle curtain – mostly white but partly purple – that the doe was barely visible. It was if she had been painted by one of the Impressionists, being made up of a mass of dots, an ethereal vision of no real substance. What was more, she obviously thought she was invisible, because she stood there for a couple of minutes, still as a rock, watching me, before giving out a single, gruff woof and bounding away.

Of course, the grass was always greener on the other side of boundary fences – and never more so than on a winter afternoon when I stealthily followed four prickets as they went up through a wood and out onto a field belonging to a neighbour. Any one of them would have made an excellent target. Although I had no right to shoot on that field, there seemed to be nobody about. Dusk was falling... I was severely tempted, but inhibited by the fact that beyond the deer, along the far side of the field, ran a dirt track between two hedges, known as Dead Man's Lane. It was not an official footpath, but it was used a good deal by walkers, and because the field was flat, a bullet that passed straight through a deer would carry on through both hedges and across the old road.

As I hesitated, the prickets moved on a few steps, creating a better angle: every yard they advanced made it safer to shoot. I was just deciding to have a go, when CRASH! I had failed to notice that Pansy, my Labrador, sitting beside me, had detected a rabbit ensconced under a heap of dead brushwood, right beneath her nose. After remaining still for three or four minutes of commendable restraint, she suddenly found the temptation too much: springing high into the air, she dropped feet-first into the sticks with a rousing impact. Out went the rabbit at 30 mph, and away went the deer at about the same speed. Dilemma solved.

Nobody had any clear idea of how many fallow there were in the area, and in an attempt to find out we formed a local deer group. I also began to arrange counts in winter. Twenty or more enthusiasts would turn out, and I organised large-scale drives, with most of the team advancing in line-abreast through plantations or older beechwoods, tapping the tree trunks with sticks so as to push the deer towards a few spotters perched in high seats, trees or other vantage points. The counts were obviously far from fool-proof: deer would often break back through the line of beaters or slip out at the sides, and there was always a risk that some would escape unseen or be counted twice. Nevertheless, the manoeuvres did give us some estimate of the population, and raised enthusiasm among those who took part.

No one was keener or more knowledgeable (or more liable to lay down the law) than old John Gassman, who had worked in the fur trade and lived in North Oxford. His German Jewish parents had taken refuge in England during the 1930s, and during the Second World War he had somehow managed to enlist in the British Army. He never lost his crunching German accent, and tended to be heavily didactic. 'Em I rright or wrrong?' he would demand, having expounded some theory about ballistics or the efficacy of lung shots; and, to save argument, we, his acolytes, would reply, 'Oh, quite right, John – absolutely.' But his experience of deer was immense, and his enthusiasm unlimited. Once in very cold weather he appeared in a waistcoat with skin on the outside and thick, dark fur inside. 'Heavens, John,' I said. 'That looks a good garment. What's it made of?'

'Heh!' he went, rubbing finger and thumb together suggestively. 'Pussy cet!' For years he had been picking off cats with a silenced .22 rifle in his garden in Headington.

We tried to involve the Thames Valley police in the activities of our group, in the hope that they would pursue poachers more keenly; but they showed little interest. Once a sergeant said heavily, 'Well – I haven't yet seen a deer on Caversham Bridge at midnight.'

'Maybe not,' I replied. 'But what would you do if you found two dead deer, still warm, in the boot of a car you'd stopped on Caversham Bridge at midnight? What would the law say to that?' The sergeant had no idea, and was obliged to admit as much.

Later the police in another division of the Thames Valley force went to the opposite extreme, and became (in my view) hell-bent on prosecuting a man who was clearly innocent. I was drawn into the affair when Mike, the accused, whom I knew as an excellent gundog trainer and handler, appealed to me for help and a character reference. The details of the case are too complicated to be rehearsed here: suffice it to say that a fallow pricket had been shot, and Mike had killed it with permission, but was accused of having poached it with an illegal weapon on land to which he had no right.

In due course he rang to ask if I would go and inspect the carcase, which had been kept as evidence and stored in the deep-freeze of the butcher's shop at a village in the Cotswolds. I agreed, and telephoned the nearest police station, at Chipping Norton, where a sergeant seemed to be in charge of the case. After making numerous difficulties, he said that I might inspect the deer only in his presence, and that the only time he could meet me at the shop was 8.30 am next Tuesday. I therefore left home at 7.00 that morning, drove across country, and reached the rendezvous five minutes early.

No policeman. Having waited half an hour, I asked the butcher if I might see the deer without any police present – whereupon he went round the back of the shop and reappeared carrying a tray of neatly wrapped frozen joints, steaks, mince and so on, packaged in plastic bags.

'That's it,' he said.

'Where's the skin?' I demanded. 'Where's the head?'

'Gone to the incinerator.'

'Who told you to skin it?'

'The police.'

'Hell!' It wasn't the butcher's fault, but I felt furious. Nothing could be inferred from the tray of meat. I couldn't tell where the beast had been hit, or what by. The evidence had been deliberately destroyed. 'You'd better put it back in the freezer,' I said, and, jumping into my car, drove straight to Chipping Norton.

The sergeant there made no apology for having missed our rendezvous. He did not even mention it. On the contrary, he started to harangue me in condescending terms, as if I was a child. 'I've got the evidence here,' he said, 'but I'm not showing it to you.'

'In that case,' I said sharply, 'what the hell's the point of my coming all this way? I have your name and number, so I might as well be going.'

That changed his tune, and he brought out his exhibits in little polythene bags – a tuft of grey fallow deer hair, and the crumpled, copper-tipped nose of a high-velocity rifle round. I saw straight away that the hair was useless as evidence, for it had not been cut off by a bullet and made into what any stalker would recognise as 'pins', with severed ends. Rather, it had been pulled out, probably on a fence or in a tussle between two bucks. The remains of the bullet did show that the deer had been killed by a legitimate weapon – which was not what the sergeant wanted to hear. I drove off in a rage, and wrote an angry letter to the Chief Constable, outlining my experience and asking if he was satisfied with the levels of honesty, efficiency and courtesy which members of his force seemed to consider adequate. He did not reply, but later I got an emollient response from some well-trained inspector who sought to explain everything away. In the end the case against Mike was dropped, ostensibly because he was dying of cancer.

A third incident reinforced my impression that police training in matters concerning sporting weapons was extremely poor. One July night another friend – another Mike, a deer-stalker and pest-controller – was sitting in his pick-up truck along with Cecil, the elderly game-keeper on the Nettlebed estate, lamping for foxes. They were on private land, with full permission to be there. Mike had loaded his .243 and for safety's sake was holding it with the barrel out the window of the driver's door when, at about 11.15, he saw headlights coming along the private road behind them.

Seconds later a police car swept across the field and pulled up alongside. The officers also were on legitimate business, for young-sters had been joy-riding and dumping vehicles on the estate. But the moment one of them saw the rifle, he lost his head and grabbed the barrel. Mike, not being sure for the moment who the newcomers were, held tight to his end of the weapon and tried to remonstrate, but the officer started shouting and radioed through to headquarters, reporting in hysterical terms that he was being threatened with a gun. When he stopped yelling abuse, Mike removed the bolt and magazine to make the weapon safe before handing it over, but he warned the man to take care, because a round sometimes stuck in the breech.

At that moment five more police cars came scorching across the field. Cecil and Mike were both handcuffed and bundled into vehicles – and Mike was just landing in the back of a car when there came an almighty report as somebody let his rifle off accidentally. Later he heard that this fellow, allegedly a firearms officer, had simply put the bolt back in place and pulled the trigger without checking whether or not the chamber was empty. Where the rifle was pointing, where the bullet went, history does not relate.

The two captives were driven into Reading and put in the cells, from which they were not released until 5 am. No charges were brought against them, but the rifle was confiscated, until, a week later, after making representations through his solicitor, Mike heard the flap of his letter box snap at 2 am one morning, and found that a hand-written note had been pushed through the door saying that he could go and collect the weapon from the police station. His wrists had been so badly damaged by having handcuffs forced onto them that he was unable to open and close his fingers, and therefore unable to work, and he had to seek the advice of a Harley Street consultant.

No offence had been committed, but no apology or compensation was forthcoming, and a phenomenal amount of police time had been wasted. If the rifle had gone off when the officer was frantically pulling at it, the outcome might have been appalling. What if it had blown his head off? Would Mike have been accused of murder or manslaughter?

In spite of these difficulties, I did my best to help the police by letting them put my name on the register of stalkers who would respond to a call-out whenever a deer was hit by a vehicle. Experience quickly taught me that if an animal as wild as a deer does not run away when humans approach, it must be very badly hurt, and that the only sensible course is to finish it off. I first saw this clearly when a friend picked up a fallow doe which he found lying beside the main road, loaded it into the boot of his car and brought it to me, begging me to do something for it. It was a beautiful young animal, and looked unharmed, with no visible injuries; so, against my better judgement,

I put it on a bed of hay in a loose box, with water in reach, and left it overnight. In the morning it was dead, and when I opened it up, I found that all its ribs on one side were broken, with the sharp ends digging into its vitals.

Answering calls to accidents always poses problems, for a mangled deer, covered in blood, with bones or intestines showing, is inevitably a distressing sight, especially for people not used to such emergencies, and anyone on the scene is liable to be upset. Great tact is needed if one arrives proposing to put the animal down. The road-side, with cars roaring past, is not a good place in which to explain that a vet – even if one were available – would probably not come out to answer a call, through uncertainty about who would pay for their services if they did, and the risk of using a lethal injection on a wild animal that is thrashing about.

There is also a problem about weapons. Although a .22 makes a perfectly adequate humane killer, and can safely administer a *coup de grâce* on or beside a thoroughfare, to shoot a deer with a rifle of that small calibre is now illegal. By law, one must use a rifle with a calibre of at least .240 – and to let off a weapon of that power on or near a public highway is definitely not recommended. A shotgun, a pistol or a captive-bolt humane killer are all better alternatives.

A full-bore rifle is certainly not suitable for use on the central reservation of a motorway, where I once had to finish off a roe doe with a broken back. The police had put out temporary speed-limit signs saying '40 mph', and their car was pulled in on the hard-shoulder with its blue lamp flashing; but drivers were taking not the slightest notice of the warnings, and were hurtling past at eighty or ninety. First I had to make a dash to the central reservation, carrying a weapon, through gaps in the oncoming stream. Then, having despatched the casualty, I had to drag it back across three lanes, with grannies on their Sunday outings turning to gawp in horror as they whizzed past. The sergeant in charge – like most policemen in my experience – was extremely squeamish and reluctant to touch the body.

Occasionally a scene of this kind can devolve into farce. One summer evening a police call came at about 8.30 pm. A deer had been knocked down at a certain small crossroads, about twenty minutes up-country. A car and two officers were in attendance, the station told me, but could I go and sort things out? Even though we were just about to have supper, I agreed, and said I would be there as soon as possible – but hardly had I set off with a rifle and ammunition when I realised that I had just downed a very considerable whisky-and-soda. What would the score be if I was breathalysed when answering a police appeal for help?

Luckily at the site a stiff breeze was blowing, and I took care to keep down-wind of the officers who greeted me. Did they notice that whenever they advanced towards me, I kept backing off, and if necessary moved sideways so that the air-flow remained safely from them to me? They told me that the injured deer was lying in a barley field just beyond a hedge, so I went to investigate; but when I looked through a gap, the animal leapt to its feet and bounded away into the nearest wood, apparently in full working order. I concluded that it had had a bang on the head, from which it had recovered, and that no further action was needed or indeed possible, as night was already falling. Still manoeuvring backwards, and sidling like a crab, I regained my car and bid the law goodnight.

One autumn morning a strange car rolled down to the back door of the house, and out got a short, stocky man with a neatly trimmed, gingery beard. 'My name's Ron LeVay,' he announced. 'I'm dying of cancer, and I don't want any fucking sympathy.'

'Oh!' I said, slightly taken aback. 'What *do* you want?'

'I want to come out stalking with you for as long as I can.'

'All right. Let's have a chat.'

Ron was in his late forties, and an experienced deer man; but by then, in the grip of Hodgkin's disease, he had become too weak to lift a shot beast into a vehicle, and so could go out only with other people. After his confrontational opening remark, he settled down over a cup of tea, and we had an enjoyable discussion, I agreed to take him out with me whenever it suited – but then, as he was about to leave, he suddenly reverted to his challenging mode and said, 'I'll come on one condition.'

'What's that?'

'That when I die, you'll have my dog.'

'What is it?'

'Come and see.'

Back at the car, he opened the tail-gate, and out jumped a beautiful black Labrador bitch. Kate, he explained, was barely a year old, and partially trained, but showing great promise. Never having owned a dog, and thinking of all the problems she would cause, I prevaricated by saying how good-looking she was, with her solid build and fine, broad head. As for taking her over – I would have to think about it.

Ron did come out with me a few times that winter. He shot several beasts, and I know he enjoyed his last season in the woods. He was with me one day when we narrowly survived a nasty accident. At the time the only vehicle I had for recovering deer was a lightweight A-35 van, which had room for several bodies in the back, but such poor clearance and traction that I could not take it along woodland rides. During a spell of bitter weather we were driving up a lane with high banks on either hand, and because the road was covered with packed snow and ice, I was proceeding with unusual caution. Suddenly a Land Rover appeared, hurtling downhill round a bend towards us. I pulled up within a yard or two, but in an instant I realised that the oncoming vehicle was out of control, going far too fast to stop. On it came, rapidly growing bigger, as if zooming in at us on a giant cinema screen. I just had time to shout 'Look out!' before it hit us head-on with an almighty crash.

Our windscreen flew back past us in a thousand pieces, cutting our faces. Ron was thrown forward so violently that the impact cracked the woodwork of his rifle, which he had been holding with the butt on the floor and the barrel resting on his shoulder. I was slightly better off, as I had braced myself on the steering wheel, but I got a severe bang on the right knee. Kate, who had been in the back but landed in the front, was unharmed.

How we summoned help – in the days before mobile telephones – or how we got home, I cannot remember. The van was a write-off: we pushed its remains into a gap in the hedge, and I never saw it again. It turned out that the Land Rover was being driven by a boy of eighteen who had just passed his test. His father, a doctor, was admirably fair in admitting responsibility on his son's behalf, and in getting his insurance to compensate me.

The money enabled me to buy a well-used mini-traveller – again, a vehicle by no means ideal for deer recovery, but all I could afford. The worst of its drawbacks was its very low clearance; the least, that it had windows all round, which made it possible for passers-by to see what was inside. One morning as we were returning from a successful expedition with two does in the back, I stopped briefly in Henley to go to the bank, leaving Ron in the passenger seat. When I returned, he claimed that 'a little old lady' had tapped on the window and asked, 'What have you got in there, young man?' To which he said he had replied, 'It's a dead donkey, madam. Unfortunately it was severely injured in an accident, and we had to put it down.' Whether or not this incident occurred, I seriously doubt. I believe it was a kind of fantasy which Ron for some reason invented.

Gradually his cancer overpowered him, and when he died Kate duly joined our household. By then she was fully trained, and heredity had armed her with the invaluable habit of lifting her nose high in the air whenever she scented deer – a reaction quite different from her head-down search for other game. Time and again she gave me early warning of deer ahead of us, and she was particularly valuable in mist or poor light.

Ron had made her a first-rate stalking dog, well able to track a wounded beast. Whenever I went out with a shotgun, she would bound around with enthusiasm and, if I let her, hunt for pheasants a few yards ahead of me; but she knew exactly what a shouldered rifle meant, and when she saw me armed in this fashion, she would walk quietly at heel without any form of restraint. In the house she was idleness personified, and when Phylla commissioned a local artist to draw her, as a present to me, the only way she could keep the sitter alert was to fire occasional shots with a .22 through an open window into the flowerbed outside. Alas, when only five Kate was killed in a thousand-to-one accident – run over during a shoot when she pursued a wounded hen pheasant across a main road; but she had shown me the immense value of stalking with a trained accomplice, and we kept her line going through successive generations.

My stalking dogs have always required minimal extra training. All Labradors seem to have an instinctive understanding of what we are doing; and provided they sit when told to, and keep quiet, they are never any trouble. When we are out on the ground, I speak to them as little as possible, because their eyes and noses tell them exactly what is happening up ahead, and instructions would be superfluous. Whenever a shot is imminent, they tremble with excitement, just as the stalker probably does; in Scotland they sometimes imitate him by crawling on their bellies in the final stages of an approach – and even if the stalk fails, their obvious enthusiasm renders the whole exercise that much more rewarding.

8

Knoydart

WHEN MY FATHER-IN-LAW decided to end his long association with Loch Choire, Phylla's brother Gerry and I rented the forest for a fortnight for two more years, bringing in contemporaries – again family and friends – to share the cost. So began a kind of tradition, in which I collected a party every year and took a week or a fortnight in one forest after another. Our last season at Loch Choire (for the time being) was enlivened by the arrival of Ronnie Macdonald, then eighteen, an energetic and amusing second stalker, whose only fault was that out of sheer keenness he tended to go too fast.

One day a member of our party, out alone with him, became irritated by the speed at which he was expected to walk, lost his temper, and without saying a word turned about and went back to the lodge. That was a selfish and nasty trick, for when Ronnie next looked round and found no one behind him, he became extremely worried, thinking his Rifle must have had a heart attack and toppled into a peat hag. Usually, though, Ronnie's optimism was buoyant, and he was given to memorable remarks – as when we were creeping round the flank of the Whip in the mist, drawn on by the persistent roaring of a stag somewhere ahead of us, and Ronnie turned round with a con- spiratorial whisper: ' We'll quieten that bugger in a moment' – which we did.

My first new target, in 1971, was the most ambitious I ever tackled. Knoydart, a peninsula on the west coast, is one of the steepest and most rugged estates in all the Highlands, and I saw it as an agreeable challenge – which indeed it turned out to be. Part of its appeal lay in the fact that there was (and is) no access by road. Unless one walks in fifteen miles through the passes of the rock-bound hinterland, known with good reason as the Rough Bounds of Knoydart, the only way to reach the scatter of houses at Inverie on the shore of Loch Nevis is by boat from the fishing port of Mallaig. In those days all 60,000 acres (100 square miles) of the forest belonged to one family, the Crosthwaite-Eyres, who owned it for twenty years.

Because it sounded so formidable, I went up on my own during the summer to make a reconnaissance, and found that the reality exceeded all expectations. As I looked landward from Mallaig, my scalp prickled at the sight of the tremendous, jagged hills across the sea loch, and during the forty-minute voyage towards them in the estate's landing-craft, the *Spanish John*, I felt I was entering another world. In the opposite direction the view was equally inspiring, with the islands of Skye, Rum and Eigg rising out of the sea in the distance.

In my warning order to members of our party I had no trouble sounding enthusiastic:

The ground is *extremely* steep, and it would be a good idea if everyone could arrive reasonably fit ... There are three stalkers, and I hope we will get two stags a day anyway, and sometimes three... The Inverie river is famous for sea trout, which weigh up to fifteen pounds ... It is alleged that there are two grouse on the whole estate, and that there is no point in chasing them. However, I do not entirely believe this... Inverie House is very comfortable. It stands on a marvellous site, right on the beach, and looks down the loch to Rum and Skye ... This is definitely not going to be a do-it-yourself holiday. There is a full-time cook, and domestic staff to clean, lay the fires, do the washing and generally run the house.

In those days an overnight Motorail service was running from London Olympia to Stirling, where we arrived with our car at 5.45 in the morning; and by this means our gang assembled on the pier at Mallaig at lunch time on a Saturday. On Knoydart itself there were a few short stretches of road – one going up Glen Dubh-Lochain, the main glen behind the house, another across to the Guseran river, on which we had the fishing rights – so we decided to take two cars over with us, and these were loaded on to the *Spanish John* slung beneath the jib of a crane. My long-term stalking accomplice David Lyon watched with some apprehension as his 3.5 Rover was swung precariously out over the dock-side and lowered on to the vessel's flat deck. As we chugged across the loch, the mountains ahead seemed to grow ever higher and more exciting.

The lodge was indeed comfortable, but it had one serious drawback, in that it lacked a drying room – a strange deficiency in a place that gets 100 inches of rainfall in a year. A more welcome surprise was to find that the house had a working telephone. How come that modern communications had been established in such a remote outpost? John Crosthwaite-Eyre, who was acting as factor for the estate, and was living in part of the lodge, told us that the line had been laid across the sea-bed from Mallaig by the previous owners, the Nall-Cain family, so that their friend and guest the Prime Minister Neville Chamberlain could keep in touch as political events were hotting up when he came to stay in 1938. Arthur Nall-Cain, second Baron Brocket, was a close associate of Chamberlain and a notorious Nazi sympathiser: a friend of Joachim von Ribbentrop, the German Ambassador in London and then Hitler's Foreign Minister, Brocket was a prominent member of the Anglo-German Fellowship, and assiduous in maintaining his contacts with leaders of the Third Reich, even after the outbreak of war in 1939.

We soon learnt that the Nall-Cains had been even less popular in Knoydart than in Whitehall. Absentee landlords, they contested the claims of the Seven Men of Knoydart, who in 1948 tried to seize land for their own use, and Brocket won his case against them when he took it to the Court of Session. Local rumour related that once, as he tried to land at Inverie, he was met by a deputation levelling shotguns at him.

Someone had warned me that Andrew Mackintosh, the Head Stalker, always known as Mac, was a dour old fellow who never spoke. This turned out to be nonsense: a stocky man, very upright, with his remaining grey hair brushed back *en brosse*, looking every inch the former company sergeant-major (which he was), he was a charming person who, when he got to know us, talked freely about the deer, the estate and its troubled history.

It was from him that I first got intimations of how badly the Brockets had treated their retainers. One morning some manoeuvre had landed us on top of Sgurr Coire Choinnichean, the dramatically steep mountain in the centre of the peninsula: he and I were standing on a ridge no more than three or four yards wide, with the sides of the hill dropping away as sharply as the roof of a Gothic cathedral on either side. It was a thrilling spot, giving us a magnificent view of the peninsula, the bay, the islands and the sea, and as we looked down Mac suddenly began, unprovoked, to tell a story.

It concerned 'young Mr Brocket', by whom I think he meant the second Baron, Arthur, who had died four years earlier. A very fine stag with a thirteen-point head had been seen around the fringes of Barrisdale Bay, at the far north-east end of the ground, and Brocket, though 'a verra puir shot', had conceived the idea that he must secure the beast's head as a trophy. One evening, after a long day, he did indeed manage to shoot the stag; but instead of leaving it where it was, and sending a boat round the coast to collect it in the morning (the normal practice), he ordered Mac to cut off its head and carry it home. This the stalker and ghillie proceeded to do – and a grim journey it was, up over a high pass in the middle of the forest, and down the other side. After a three-hour trek, during which Brocket walked behind them, neither speaking nor offering to lend a hand, they reached the lodge at 9 pm – and Mac finished his narrative with a sudden explosive twist that hinted at years of anger and frustration: 'He goes to the back door, and "Good night" he says – *and that's all the bugger would say.*'

Mac's best asset was his uphill pace. At Loch Choire we had been spoilt by the fact that the lodge stands 700 feet above sea-level, and that the hills around it are not particularly high or steep. Stalking at Knoydart, we started from sea-level every morning, and almost invariably climbed to 2000 feet before we were in business. Mac's way of gaining height was to proceed at what seemed, to begin with, a ridiculously slow pace, with one foot plodding laboriously past the other; yet his tortoise-like advance proved extraordinarily effective, and always got the party to the required height in good time without leaving anyone exhausted.

The second stalker, Sandy Morrison, a much younger man, was quite the opposite. Always in a hurry, he was inclined to break into a run at moments of excitement, in spite of repeated requests to slow down. One day he and I were coming round the top of a big corrie full of rocks when we spotted a stag some way below us and well ahead. The beast was preoccupied with thoughts of rutting, and was throwing up lumps of peat with its antlers; also, it was facing away from us, and had no inkling of our presence. Nevertheless, Sandy at once began advancing at a fast lope, and by the time we flopped down onto a rock within range, we were both panting hard. As I tried to settle my rifle into a comfortable position, he let out a burst of instructions that began slowly but ended in an accelerating rush. 'Take your time, Sir, take your time,' he purred, and then, without any pause, 'Hurry-upshootmanhe'soff!'

'Rubbish!' I said. 'He's not off at all.' So I took my time and shot the stag dead.

Stalking with Mac was much more deliberate, but no less exciting. One day he, I and Labrador Kate (as he called her) had reached a considerable height when the mist came in on us. The rut was on, and from a distance we had seen a lot of activity near the top of a steep face. Approaching cautiously from a flank, we came over a crest in the cloud, and although for the time being we could see nothing, continual roaring from several stags left no doubt that the deer were very close in front of us. For a while we continued to creep forward, descending slightly, until the stags sounded as if they were within touching distance, and we could hear the clatter of hooves as deer skittered about over the stones.

'We'll give it a minute,' Mac breathed. 'See if it'll clear.'

I settled down in a firing position, and for perhaps half an hour we lay there, with the mist drifting silently across us from right to left and fine moisture settling on our clothes and hands. Kate sat behind me bolt upright, trembling with excitement, as beads of water gathered on her eyebrows and whiskers. The action close in front of us was non-stop: from the racket we could tell that two or three stags were on the go, and one particular beast was making more noise than the rest – but we could not see a thing.

Then at last I suddenly spotted something to our left – a great, black object which seemed to loom out of the mist, as large as a double-decker bus.

'Christ!' I exclaimed. 'What's that?'

'It's the stag! Shoot, man. Shoot!'

The stag was black as night, from rolling in peat, and facing us head on. Swivelling to my left, I aimed at the base of his neck and squeezed the trigger – and down he went like a stack of bricks.

Whether it was just a fluke of timing, or something to do with the percussion of the shot, I shall never know. Whatever the cause, at that instant the mist abruptly lifted a few feet, and suddenly beneath the grey ceiling right over our heads we could see that the entire hillside below us was alive with running deer, streaming from left to right. Later we reckoned there must have been three hundred of them.

Left to myself, I would never have analysed that avalanche of animals; but Mac was watching coolly through binoculars, and a moment later said, 'Yon light-coloured stag in the middle. If he stops, belt him.'

I spotted the beast he meant – a very pale, almost pink stag with a big body, cantering fast, escorted by droves of hinds and calves flying alongside. Seconds later he ran up onto a knoll, stopped, turned to look backwards and stood clear, broadside-on. Without waiting for any further instruction I laid the cross-hairs on him, half-way up the body behind the shoulder, and fired. He buckled and spun round at the shot, but started to run again.

'Watch him! snapped Mac. 'Ye've hit him low. We'll need to get down there.' But before we were on our feet he cried, 'Oh, hell! The dog's away!'

She was, too. Goaded into action by the excitement, Kate had broken ranks and was hurtling down the hill towards the wounded beast, disappearing into hollows, popping into view again. There was no point in whistling or shouting. No power on earth would have stopped her. I watched in horror as she charged straight towards the stag, all too well aware that if she tried to lay hold of it, it might despatch her with one sweep of its antlers. Although I had twice seen her pull down a wounded fallow doe, she had never taken on a big buck, still less a stag.

Yet by some miracle of instinct she knew exactly what to do. Instead of putting in a direct attack, she pulled up some twenty yards short of the beast and ran round it in a circle, barking continuously. The stag, turning again and again to face her, was anchored to the spot, and we had no trouble approaching to within fifty yards and giving it another bullet. Only when we looked back to where the body of the first stag was still lying did I realise that I had fired at the second from a range of 300 yards, and that in the heat of the moment I had failed to make allowance for the bullet dropping.

The variety of stalking at Knoydart exceeded anything we had known before. Parties could start up Glen Dubh-Lochain, the central glen, or go round the coast by boat, either northabout, to Barrisdale

Bay, at the head of Loch Hourn, or southabout to Finiskaig, at the end of Loch Nevis, and work their way back towards Inverie. The precipitous steepness of the hills was also in a different league, and nobody could complain about lack of exercise. Often a day ended with our dragging a stag out into the shallows of the sea loch and the *Spanish John* coming to meet us.

Our fishermen and women, on the other hand, had a lean time. There were plenty of salmon and sea trout in the river – we could see them every day – but attempts to catch them by conventional means proved so futile that, with the agreement and participation of John Crosthwaite-Eyre, we netted one of the pools. The result was amazing: a miraculous draft that brought up maybe fifty fish of various sizes. We put most of them back, but kept any which had been damaged – and John took the biggest off to the south, leaving our own larder well stocked with the smaller fry. One consolation for the fishers was Loch Bhromisaig, 1400 feet above the lodge on the south side of the glen – a wonderful place to spend a day. The stiff climb to it was usually well rewarded, for a boat was kept up there, and the water was teeming with good-sized trout.

One of the stars in our party was Gerry's latest girlfriend, Kate Bail-lieu, a strking Australian blonde, six foot tall, very good-looking, and with such a hint of the predator about her that when she overslept in the morning, and I asked one or other of the men to go and wake her up, all made excuses to avoid the errand. Gerry, having worked for some time in Bahrain, had acquired a penchant for wearing Arab dress – so it was no great surprise to members of the family when two tall figures appeared in sheikhly robes at a ceilidh, held in the village hall built by John's father. What did startle us all was the revelation that the alleged Arabs were both in drag: the sheikh was unveiled as Kate, and the begum as Gerry. The ceilidh was supposed to be alcohol-free, but everyone smuggled in bottles of whisky, and by about 11 pm the fiddler who led the reels had sunk into the most extraordinary attitude: although he was still seated on a chair, his upper body was horizontal, and he was still playing all-out, his face inches from the floor.

Enchanted by the beauty of Knoydart, we returned next summer for a week as guests of our lifelong friends Val and Elizabeth Fleming. We stayed at Glaschoille, a spacious house on the north shore of Loch Nevis, and the holiday was principally for the benefit of our young children; but Val and I hatched a plan to ascend Sgurr-na-Ciche, the mountain sometimes known as 'The Matterhorn of Scotland' whose conical summit rose in splendid and challenging isolation beyond the eastern end of the loch.

The day proved quite a tough one. After a five-star breakfast at 6.30 am we rode on borrowed bicycles round to the pier at Inverie, where Angus, a local fisherman, picked us up in his small boat and ferried us down the loch to Finiskaig. It was a miserable morning, with the cloud right down and drizzle falling; but once the expedition was launched, there was no turning back.

No sooner had Angus put us ashore in his dinghy than we started to climb. Up we went into the mist, and within a few minutes visibility was zero. The higher we went, the harder the going became. From a distance the mountain had looked like a smooth cone, with the sides tapering neatly towards the top, but the reality, seen from close quarters, was entirely different. We kept coming to vertical rock faces which disappeared into the fog above, and we had to make one detour after another to circumvent them. At least it was not cold. On the contrary, we were soon streaming with sweat; but the mist was extremely disorientating, and I had to make frequent checks with a compass to be sure in which direction we were heading. We were climbing blind, and only when we suddenly blundered on to a trig stone, and found that there was no more hill above us, did we realise that we had reached the summit. It was 11.15, and after making a major effort, we were hugely disappointed to have no view of any kind.

Having allowed ourselves one sandwich from our pieces, we started down. Our return journey was even more strenuous. First we had to descend the mountain, which we did by following an old sheep-wall and fence down to the Carnach River; then, after a stretch up the burn, we turned left – south-west – on to a zig-zag path that took us over a pass and into the head of Glen Meadail. At 2 pm, Val changed his shirt and we ate the rest of our lunch, before going on down the long decline and emerging into Glen Dubh-Lochain, the main glen behind Inverie House. There our bikes were awaiting us, and we were soon back at Glaschoille, lowering cup after cup of tea. We had walked some sixteen miles and climbed from sea-level to 3410 feet – not to mention the second ascent into Glen Meadail. Needless to say, in the evening the clouds lifted, and the summit of Sgurr-na-Ciche stood out in perfect profile, pink and grey against a clear sky.

Later, I was glad to find our enthusiasm for Knoydart reflected by Arthur and Catherine Bowlby, who bought the estate in 1895 and kept it for more than thirty years. At their invitation the celebrated Scottish bird artist Archibald Thorburn went up in about 1908 and did a port-folio of fine landscape watercolours which lay undiscovered until they were found and came to the market nearly a hundred years later.

Another of the Bowlbys' friends was the portrait artist Philip de László, who painted a charming little picture of the Knoydart stalkers, and to whom Catherine wrote on 22 October 1910:

The birches up the glens have all turned, and Knoydart glows still more. I have been out on the hills seven times with the ghillies, and after ptarmigan, and whilst they pursue their path of killing, I sit on the tops and feel there is nothing between me and the clouds but all that is beautiful, spaceless and eternal. I am so glad you liked being up here, for Knoydart, its hills and its ever-changing colours are as near perfection in my eyes as any place on earth can be.

9

Stonor to Kathmandu

IN THE CHILTERNS THE NEED for culling kept increasing. To avoid wearing out the barrel of the .300 – which in any case was really too powerful for fallow – I decided I needed a new rifle, and at Holland & Holland, in London, I found one which I thought would suit me perfectly: a Ruger .243, a light, accurate weapon with a short barrel, which would make it easy to handle in woodland. Another advantage was that its relatively small bullets, 100 grain or 80 grain, would do less damage to deer carcases.

Having set up the purchase and obtained the necessary alteration of my firearms certificate from the Thames Valley police, I arranged to collect the rifle one morning on my way to work. At that time I was keeping a bicycle at Paddington Station and riding to Fleet Street, so it was easy to drop in on the gunmakers in Bruton Street, Mayfair, and collect my new weapon, which I slung on my back in a tan-coloured canvas cover. Taking one of my normal commuter routes, I crossed Regent Street, wove my way through Soho and came down into the Strand.

There I noticed that a great many uniformed police seemed to be on the move, pacing slowly about the pavements. In the Aldwych they were even thicker on the ground, and at the top end of Fleet Street they were positively swarming. With my mind focused on the day's work, I took no particular notice, and stopped, as usual, outside Mick's Café, on the left-hand side of the road about a hundred yards short of the *Telegraph* building, propping my bike on the kerb while I went in to buy a carton of milk for our coffee.

As I was about to go through the door I became aware of a presence close behind me. Turning round, I found a policeman confronting me, about six inches away.

'What's that you've got on your back?' he demanded.

'A rifle.'

'Why are you carrying it?'

'I've just bought it.'

'Where are you going?'

'To the *Telegraph*. I work there,'

'Have you got a certificate for the weapon?'

'Certainly.' I had the document in the breast pocket of my jacket, and handed it over.

The copper turned away abruptly so that his back was facing me. Then he opened the envelope, unfolded the certificate, stared at it, and asked over his shoulder, 'How tall are you?'

'Six two.'

'What's your second name?'

'Duff.'

He turned back to look at me, as if to confirm the information (which was on the certificate anyway), but he seemed rather agitated – and he nearly went airborne a second or two later when he asked, 'You haven't got any ammunition with you?'

'Yes I have,' I said, 'I've got a hundred rounds.'

'Where is it?'

'In my briefcase on the back of the bike.'

'Jesus Christ! Get in there!'

Ushering – almost pushing – me into the café, to the astonishment of other customers, he called urgently for reinforcements over his radio. Within seconds three colleagues bustled in, and I was surrounded – but when I offered to hand the rifle over to one of them, he seemed horrified by the idea of touching it, and waved it away. Soon I and my escort were marching down Fleet Street, with one of them wheeling my bike. At No 135 we all went into the grandiose, hideous 1930s marble hall of the *Telegraph* building and stood there while the law debated what action to take. My colleagues coming in on their way into work were agreeably surprised by the sight of me – as they thought – being taken into custody.

I suggested I should deposit the rifle at Snow Hill police station, round the corner, and surrender it for the duration. But no – that was not acceptable. I offered to lock it in a cupboard. Still no good. Finally it was agreed that I should hand over the bolt and the ammunition to the newspaper's accountants, who would lock it in their safe, and that I would keep the disabled weapon in my own office. With that settled, the coppers dispersed and I went up in the lift. Only then did I discover what all the fuss had been about. Alert as ever, I had failed to realise that this was the day of the service of thanksgiving for victory in the Falklands War, to be held in St Paul's Cathedral, and that a cavalcade of vehicles ferrying most of the royal family would be coming past at any moment.

Luckily I had not committed any crime, and in the evening I biked back to Paddington, carrying the re-assembled rifle, without fuss. Admittedly security in those days was nothing like as tight as it is now; but I still believe that if I had approached Fleet Street down Shoe Lane, or one of the other rat-runs coming in from the north (as I often did), I could have slipped in through the back door of the *Telegraph* building unobserved, and gained a perfect sniper's position at the window of my third-floor office.

The new .243 was soon in service. Next to the north, beyond the Hambleden ground, lay Stonor, once another magnificent estate, but now sadly reduced by sales of outlying land. Its centrepiece was, and remains, Stonor Park, which has belonged to the family of that name for more than 800 years – and a lovelier setting could hardly be imagined. The 230 acres of parkland lie in a natural bowl, set wide and deep into the surrounding hills, with open grass on its lower reaches, and beechwoods massed on the curving steeper slopes above. The house – long, low and faced with pink brick and flint, with its own flint-walled chapel attached to the eastern end – sits comfortably across the hill, on the left as you go up the drive, and it looks out over the grass-land, on which the resident herd of fallow deer is often grazing. For centuries the house has been a centre of Roman Catholicism, particularly associated with the Jesuit priest and martyr Edmund Campion, who in 1581 took refuge in an attic room, where his book *Decem Rationes* (Ten Reasons), attacking the Anglican Church, was secretly printed.

The deer have been there as long as the Stonor family, and for generations they have been one of the park's chief attractions; but when I began culling, at the owners' invitation, they were out of control. The boundary fence had fallen into disrepair, and many of them had escaped into the conifer plantations on top of the hill, where they were breeding freely. The numbers were seriously large. Late one night a man reeled out of the Drover, the pub on the road that ran along the upper edge of the plantations, and a few seconds later crashed back into the bar shouting, 'Christ almighty! I've just seen three hundred pairs of bloody eyes, all moving!'

From their secure base among the trees, the deer were storming out at night to raid the crops on nearby fields, thereby inciting much hostility from local farmers. They were also damaging the conifers – partly by browsing but mainly by beating them up during the onset of the rut, when bucks would mark their territories and vent their frustration by thrashing off the branches with their antlers.

Major culls were needed – but matters were not easy to arrange, for the head of the family, Sherman, Lord Camoys, though friendly and gentle, was indecisive, and his wife Jeanne was difficult, to say the least. Small and slender, with huge eyes and the looks of a beautiful but dangerous doll, she antagonised almost everyone with whom she had dealings, and was particularly vicious in her hatred of most of her own five children. She and Sherman both took an intensely pro-prietorial attitude towards the deer, which they rightly regarded as one of the park's great glories. Both knew that a big cull was needed, but neither liked the idea. Both were anxious to restore the park fence, so that the herd could be contained and properly managed; but they had no money to spend on repairs, and for years nothing had been done.

Somehow I secured the task of reducing numbers. Jeanne announced that I was her verderer, and for the next few seasons I had unlimited stalking: eighty deer one year, one hundred the next. I built several high seats, some propped against trees on the outskirts of woods, others free-standing in the open, at points where a massacre of the young trees had left clear glades in the forestry. Erecting a free-standing seat is rather like attempting the Indian rope trick: it is easy enough to cobble together a couple of A-frames out of slender poles lying on the ground, but quite another matter to get them upright and attached to each other so that they give mutual support. Ropes, ladders and a Land Rover or tractor were all essential items of equip-ment. Commercially made seats made of steel or aluminium were available, but as they cost several hundred pounds each, they were beyond our budget.

I sold the venison on behalf of the estate, and opened a bank account into which I put the proceeds, my plan being that the money should go towards restoration of the park fence. The trouble was that prices were miserable: we could usually get no more than one shilling (5 p) a pound, which meant that a pricket was worth about £3.50, a doe only £3. Not that all the carcases went to the butcher: Jeanne would occasionally issue a peremptory call for venison, so I would skin a doe and take it to the house. I once went to the back door with a carcase on my shoulder, and, on getting no response to the bell, proceeded into the medieval kitchen. There I disturbed a very senior-looking rat, which lolloped the length of the refectory table before jumping off and disappearing into the gloom at floor level.

Another occasional customer was the landlord of the Stonor Arms – then a superior hostelry in the village, with a reputation for excellent food. One evening at about eight o'clock I hung a carcase in the chill room at the back of the yard, and went into the kitchen to recover the plate on which I had brought the liver. As I waited, a flustered young chef suddenly appeared saying, 'Bloody hell! I've had *another* order for lamb chops *chasseur*' – with which he dived into a deep-freeze, pulled out a stick of frozen lumps, stuffed it down among some soapy dishes in the sink, turned the hot tap on it and went away to do something else. I never ate in that pub again.

Eventually Tommy Stonor, the elder son, who had inherited some of his mother's steel but also his father's gentleness, found the money to rebuild the fence, and we arranged for deer-leaps to be left open at strategic points, so that animals which had been excluded could jump down a drop and join or rejoin the main herd, but could not get out again. This meant that the free population was reduced, but that large and ever-increasing numbers of deer were enclosed – and a magnificent sight they made in that setting, especially the great bucks, with their spotted coats and widely palmated antlers. By any standards they were strong deer, and as they grazed in the open opposite the ancient house, they perfectly complemented the scene, as their ancestors had done since the Middle Ages and before.

And yet, splendid though they looked, a major effort was needed to reduce their numbers. With the help of a young park-keeper, Steve Poole, who was taken on by the family, I culled nearly 200 beasts that first year. It was no easy task, for as soon as we started shooting, the deer would either seek refuge in a patch of rhododendrons at one top corner of the park, or else coalesce into a dense mass out in the centre of the grassland. Perhaps it was an age-old instinct, inherited from the days when wolves were still their main enemy, which told them that keeping close together offered some protection. At any rate, their tactics were effective, for by standing bunched, constantly twitching and shifting about, they made it very difficult to single out individual targets: because a rifle bullet would generally pass straight through one beast, we could not risk wounding another beyond it, and so had to hold our fire. A further hazard was that a public footpath ran through the park, along the slope opposite the house, and although we put up warning notices at the entrances on days when culling was in progress, asking people to stay clear for their own safety, determined hikers were still liable to assert their rights and walk through.

We found that our best method was to deploy one or two extra riflemen at key points, either in high seats or concealed at the base of tree trunks, and keep moving the deer round. In spite of the difficulties, we often managed to cull fifteen in a session – and by the time we had collected the bodies, carted them back to the larder, gralloched them and cleaned them out, we felt we had done a good day's work.

All the time we were trying not just to reduce numbers, but also to be selective: to take out bucks with weak heads, and does that looked old or in poor condition. At one stage a few of the deer appeared to be suffering from some disorder that made them giddy: they would stagger about and even fall over – and these, of course, were prime targets, although in the end it turned out that our worries were unnecessary. A post-mortem performed on a buck which became unsteady and then expired revealed that it had died of alcohol poisoning, brought on by a surfeit of crab apples.

Another consideration was that the owners preferred fallow of the brightly spotted menil variety; many in the herd were that colour, but some were grey and others almost black, and although we concentrated on removing as many of the dusky ones as possible, their genes seemed to overpower those of the lighter animals, so that the dark colours kept recurring. There were also, at any one time, four or five pure white does, which invested the herd with a certain element of romance: these we left alone – but again nature seemed determined to defeat us, for although the white ladies did occasionally throw white fawns, their offspring were generally brown or grey. For several years a handsome white buck was seen about the hills outside the park, and I kept hoping he would jump in; but he was too wily for that, and in the end he was shot by a notorious, titled poacher, who boasted about his triumph in the pub.

One autumn in the approach to the rut, as a means of increasing revenue, we arranged with a lively Irish sporting agent, Pat Synnott, for each of two German clients to shoot a medal-class buck. A rendezvous was set for 7 am at the park gates on a Monday morning; and during the week before that Steve Poole and I identified two old stagers which we thought would do for the trophy-hunters. Both animals still had good heads, but they were past their prime, and would be well out of the way before the rut started. Unfortunately, on the Friday the larger of the two animals, known to us as the Big Fellow, got into a fight with a rival, and Steve saw it sustain such a heavy charge in the ribs that it was flung into the air and crash-landed on its side on the drive going up through the park. Thereafter, on Saturday and Sunday, he did not see it any more, and we feared it might have died.

When the visitors arrived promptly at the park gates on a frosty morning, I briefed them as best I could in German. Then we split into two parties, one going left-handed with Steve round the perimeter of the park, and the other with me, right-handed, with Pat bringing up the rear in a natty, three-piece green tweed suit.

I had advanced barely a couple of hundred yards when I noticed a movement in some deep bracken over on my right. Binoculars revealed one antler of the Big Fellow. Clearly he was lying down, and the peculiar swaying motion suggested that he was mortally injured. I glanced at the German, who luckily was looking the other way. Then I said quietly, '*Ein Moment, bitte,*' and dropped back for a quick conference with Pat.

'The buck we want is over there,' I whispered, 'but he's been injured and he's nearly dead. I can't let your man shoot that.'

'Ah, God, he will. He'll shoot anything. Carry on. He doesn't care about the stalk. It's only a gold medal he's wanting.'

So I withdrew, and came forward again in a ridiculously over-elaborate and cautious approach. 'I just caught a glimpse of something in this corner,' I told the German. '*Vorsicht!*' Presently I made out the big antler again, and from a distance of forty yards I gave a whistle. With an obvious effort the old buck raised his head, and the German shot him neatly through the neck. He was thrilled with his trophy, and even more delighted when I told him he could shoot another beast with poor antlers, for free. When I gralloched the Big Fellow, I found that all his ribs were broken along one side, and the ends had punctured his lungs. He would soon have died anyway, but his quick exit had earned the park £250.

For a while I took on the management of another park, at Fawley, close to Henley, the home of Bill McAlpine, of the building family. This was smaller than Stonor, and held fewer deer – but still they needed culling, and operations were complicated by the fact that, besides the deer and a full-scale steam railway, the park contained a herd of wallabies. It was disconcerting, to say the least, as I was taking aim at a fallow doe, to have one of them hurtle across the telescopic sight in long bounds. When some of the herd escaped, they took happily to the surrounding countryside – and early one morning a postman thought he was hallucinating when he saw a kangaroo-type animal hopping towards him up the Market Place in Henley.

Stonor, however, remained the centre of my operations. In the spring of 1976 Sherman had died, aged sixty-two, leaving Jeanne in sole command of the house and estate – a situation by no means to the liking of local people. One afternoon I was helping build a pheasant release-pen in a wood a few miles away when I asked our under-keeper, Alan Butler – formerly an employee of the Stonors – what the funeral had been like.

'Cor,' he said, 'there was hundreds of 'em stood out in the rain, all down the bloody park.' He paused, pushing back his hat, then went on, 'The old bugger was there. Had a black bloody net throwed over her head, so bloody thick you couldn't hardly *see* her.' Again there was a pause, before he added with great vehemence, 'CHRIST she is a bugger!'

'Ah, go on,' said Cecil, our own gamekeeper. 'She can't be that bad.'

'She bloody is,' went Alan. 'I tell yer ...' and off he launched into a tirade of grievances, frequently employing a word beginning with f.

For the time being I remained in favour, and my involvement with the Stonors took a curious direction through their association with the royal family of Nepal. When Crown Prince Birendra was sent to Eton in the 1960s, Tommy had been appointed his mentor, and a firm friendship had grown up between the two clans. I knew about this, and I had taken Tommy's advice before going on a trek in the Himalayas in 1974. Even so, I was slightly startled when, in the winter of 1976, a telephone call came from Jeanne, more or less ordering me to take a visiting Nepalese prince out to shoot a buck in the park. By then Birendra had succeeded his father as King, and the visitor was his youngest brother, Prince Dhirendra, about twenty-five at the time.

I drove across feeling slightly apprehensive, my anxiety exacerbated by the fact that a six-inch blanket of snow was lying on the hills. How should I treat this exotic visitor? Could he shoot? How would he react to the wintry weather? Would he have any of the right kit? I found a dapper young man, not nearly as soft as I had feared, and sensibly dressed for the outdoors. When I proposed that he should fire my rifle at a target before we went out to stalk, he readily agreed, and he made no fuss about lying down on a patch of snow that I had trampled. He was obviously familiar with weapons, and fired a couple of accurate shots. Nor did he hesitate when, on our way round the park, we dislodged a moderate, middle-aged buck from a snow-laden holly bush: when I handed him the rifle and said, 'Go on – shoot', he killed it expertly.

That little episode led to a far more distant expedition in 1984, when, through Tom, I arranged to interview King Birendra for *The Sunday Telegraph*. So remote were most parts of Nepal, and so poor were communications in the mountain kingdom, that the monarch had taken to establishing camps in forward areas so that he himself could inspect development projects. In the winter of my visit he had opted for a region in the south, towards the border with India, and it was there that I was due to meet him.

Arriving in Kathmandu, I found myself in the charge of Hemanta Mishra, head of the country's wildlife department – a delightful fellow, lively, quick-minded and highly knowledgeable, whose fluent English had been given an extra dimension by a season's work as a ghillie in the Scottish Highlands. There he had picked up an astonishing variety of swear-words, which he deployed freely in whatever language he was speaking. Thus in the middle of a conversation with the King's ADC, over a terrible radio link, he kept interrupting volleys of what sounded like curried Italian with '*Oh-for-fuck's-sake!*' before breaking back into Nepali.

The upshot of his exchanges was that I would have to wait a few days for my audience; so we drove down into the jungles of Chitwan, where he had been fitting rhinos and tigers with radio-collars and tracking their movements, to discover more about their territorial habits. His immediate project was to capture a rhino which had managed to divest itself of its collar, and to equip it with a new one.

We had scarcely arrived at the camp when he said, 'You've shot hundreds of deer, Duff. *You* shoot this bloody rhino.'

The next I knew, I was sitting on the neck of an elephant, hard up against the back of the *phanit*, or driver (the equivalent of the Indian *mahout*), holding a Cap-Chur dart gun in my left hand and hanging on to a rope collar with my right. Rich smells were all around, though whether they emanated from elephant or driver, it was not easy to determine.

The gun was loaded with a hefty hypodermic missile – a needle as thick as a four-inch nail, backed by a tube of anaesthetic – but since it was accurate over only a short distance, my instructions were not to fire until we were within thirty yards of the target, and then to aim for the rhino's backside.

First we had to find the right beast. It was a glorious winter's day, with the temperature about 70°F, the sun agreeably hot, and

Himalayan peaks glittering white on the horizon ninety miles to the north. Our five elephants crunched their way through bushes and scattered trees in line-abreast formation, steered by the drivers digging their big toes into the soft folds behind their ears. Peacocks rocketed up out of the scrub in little coveys, climbing powerfully, and the occasional rhino lumbered away – but it was half an hour before we found the one we wanted, identifiable by a tear in his left ear.

As the elephants moved in on him, he peered round suspiciously, but stood his ground. Then my mount, having moved steadily enough so far, began to swing its trunk violently and weave from side to side, not caring for the proximity of the two-ton creature in front of it. To align my weapon, I had to keep changing sides, lifting it over the head of the *phanit* and lowering in on to his left shoulder, then back on to his right. To the man's credit, he did not flinch, but he could not stop his mount jigging about, and it was hardly surprising that when I eventually pulled the trigger, the dart hit the rhino not in the immense buttock at which I was aiming, but in the root of his tail.

Away he went with a rush, aware that something untoward had occurred, but not certain what. 'Fucking hell!' shouted Hemanta. 'I don't know if that'll work. I've never seen one hit there before.' But work it did. After covering thirty or forty yards at a speed amazing for so heavy a creature, the rhino stopped, began to sway backwards and forwards, and slowly subsided on to his front, with his head and neck turned to one side, and his forelegs folded neatly under him.

All the humans bar the *phanits* dismounted. Now speed was of the essence, for if the great beast lay still too long, his sheer weight might compress his internal organs and kill him. Two men struggled to fix the heavy radio-collar round his neck. A visiting American scientist took measurements, principally of his canine teeth. Other men poured water over him to keep him from over-heating. When I punched the fallen giant on his shoulder, I understood for the first time the true import of the word 'pachyderm'. Thick-skinned he was: the armour plate which covered him was so substantial that I could scarcely feel the flesh underneath; and when, for the benefit of the scientist, I tried to turn his head from one side to the other, I found I could not move it. Three of us were needed to roll that part of him over, and someone said that his head and neck alone probably weighed 1500 lbs.

After only eight or nine minutes the various tasks were complete. With the rest of us back on our elephants, Hemanta administered an antidote and himself scrambled aloft. A minute or two later Radio Duff, as he was now called, stirred, struggled briefly, lurched to his feet and stumbled away, with his collar giving out a two-tone signal which would pin-point his movements over the months to come.

Next morning, fired up by this success, Hemanta announced that we would try to dart a tigress, who had also shed her radio. Soon after first light one of the trackers attached to the camp had spotted the animal going into a stand of thick grass, in which she was clearly going to lie up for the day, so arrangements were made to drive the patch with elephants. The grass was ten or twelve feet tall, and along the dusty tracks which ran down the sides of it, white tapes were hung on bushes, converging in a V, the hope being that if the tigress tried to break out on one of the flanks, the tapes would turn her and push her forward to the point of the V, where a single large tree stood in a glade, with clear ground beneath it, offering a vantage-point for a dart-gunner.

In mid-morning Hemanta and I were decanted from elephant-back into the lower branches of the tree. Neither of us was feeling particularly robust, as we had hit the Gurkha rum punches the night before, and now we had a brief argument about who was to shoot; but I persuaded him that he, with far the greater experience, had better have the dart-gun – and in any case I was not sorry to scramble higher into the branches. Tigers, I knew, do not normally climb, but this one was obviously going to be put under some stress, and I wasn't sure how she might react.

Ten elephants formed a beating line some 500 yards away from us, and the beginning of the drive was signalled by an amazing outburst of noise: the men on top, four or five to each beast, began to shout, hoot, howl, blow horns, beat drums and rattle tin cans full of stones. The elephants contributed to the din by swatting down great swathes of the grass with their trunks: every step they took was accompanied by a heavy rushing or crashing sound, almost a roar.

As the drive closed in towards us, things became intolerably exciting. We were back in the days of the Raj, when immense tiger shoots were laid on for visiting royalty, and elephants deployed in a wide circle gradually closed in towards the centre of the beat. Except that Hemanta and I were up a tree, rather than in a howdah, everything was exactly the same: the hot sun, the tall grass, the banshee howling and rattling of the beaters, the knowledge that a tiger was close at hand.

Suddenly, out to our left, one of the elephants screamed – a sound of jolting harshness, as if a giant had ripped a sheet of corrugated iron in half. Clearly the beast had seen or smelt the quarry. The human cacophony intensified. Seconds later another elephant screamed, straight in front of us, then another, further to the right. The tigress was coursing along the line, trying to break back. I found I was holding my breath. Any moment now, she must appear.

On came the line. *Swish! Crash!* went the elephants, smashing down the brittle stalks. Soon, although we could not see them, they were only forty or fifty yards away. Still the tigress did not show. We had hoped she would come forward early and slowly, trying to slip away; but by then she was trapped in a small and steadily decreasing area, with huge pressure building behind her, and it was clear that when she did break cover, she would come like the wind.

Sure enough: at the last moment she bolted. All I saw was a blur of movement across the open ground beneath our tree – a streak the colour of apricot jam, as she flashed across the glade in a couple of bounds. I saw enough of her to tell that she looked wonderfully sleek and fit, but Hemanta had no chance of darting her. He did not even have time to align the rifle, let alone take aim. In a flash she was under us and gone, and behind us one of the trackers saw her leap high over the white tape as she soared away to freedom.

Two days later we proceeded to the Monarch's camp, where we were met by the Gurkha colonel in charge of administration. He had allocated a tent to Hemanta and me, but something was obviously worrying him, and after a few minutes he came out with it. My bed, he feared, was too short. I would be uncomfortable. I assured him I would be fine, as we had brought our own sleeping bags. Still the colonel seemed unhappy – and what should we find when we came back from supper, but that carpenters had been summoned and my bed had been extended: the six-foot sheet of plywood, sitting on trestles, had been replaced by two four-foot sheets cobbled together, so that I had eight feet of plywood on which to stretch out.

Hemanta warned me that when King Birendra went walkabout, as now, he took his whole cabinet with him, so that there was a good chance that if I repaired to the communal latrine in the morning, I might find myself perching next to the Prime Minister. Luckily I escaped that embarrassment, and the King, who received me in a very fine office tent, was friendly, welcoming and exceedingly civilised. In the course of a fascinating interview I asked if he thought the day would come when roads were built to all the villages in Nepal. His answer was 'No – that will never happen, because the terrain is impossibly steep.'

Back in England, I hit trouble. Scarcely a day after my return Jeanne was on the telephone from Stonor, accusing me of having shot four bucks in the park without telling her. When I assured her that I had shot none at all – that I hadn't even been there – she would not believe me.

'My evidence is impeccable,' she insisted. 'I want a full explanation.'

What finished her, I think, was *my* evidence. 'I couldn't have shot anything,' I told her. 'I've just come back from Kathmandu.'

Kathmandu! Ye gods! That was *her* territory, and I claimed to have been there! *And* to have met the King! It was too much. 'You can clear off now!' she cried. 'Send me a cheque for all the money you've got in the account. I don't want you here any more.'

Stonor Park – (*above*) the house and (*left*) one of the homemade high seats

(*above*) Fallow fawn and (*below*) sika in summer coats

Looking up Loch Choire

Above Loch Etive: Tim Healy (*right*) with the author, his wife Phyllida and Pansy the Labrador.

(*above*) Glenaladale and (*below*) the Duchess of Bedford's encampment
in Glenfeshie, now all-but obliterated

(*above*) Loch Choire and (*below*) a mishap with the Argo on Meall-na-Caillich, Loch Choire

(*above*) The Mugger at Screebe (*below*) the head of the Pirate

Conaglen – Chris Ogilvy spying

On top of the world: Davy McAuley (*right*) above Corrie Reidh, Glenadale

Conaglen: (*above*) at the target, Donald Kennedy on the right;
(*below*) Donald Kennedy at the head of the glen

(*above*) Sea King to the rescue of the Dutchman in Glenkinglass and
(*below*) Robin Maclean at the oars with the *Cathula* in the background, Ardtornish

Conaglen: (*above*) elegance on the hill, left to right, Katy Stewart-Smith, Christy Stewart-Smith and Donald Kennedy; (*below*) John McGaskell (ghillie) bringing home a stag

Soon afterwards she began ringing round in search of a replacement verderer. Two of my friends received calls, but when she said, 'I need someone to look after my deer,' both replied, 'Well – the best person lives very close to you – and that's Duff.'

'Not having him!' she snapped – and that, for the time being, was that.

My article about Nepal was published across two pages of *The Sunday Telegraph* in 1985, timed to coincide with a visit to Kathmandu by our own Queen and Prince Philip, who were on their way to Australia. As the Queen greeted the world's only Hindu monarch on his own territory, she told him with delight that a wonderful article about him had appeared that very day in one of the English newspapers. Little did she (or he) know that, by far-sighted planning, the author of it had secured himself a memorable winter holiday.

For a while it seemed that the Stonors' time in their family home was coming to an end, when Jeanne, increasingly eccentric and malevolent, put first the furniture and then the house itself on the market. By various stratagems Tommy managed to gain control of the house and park, while his mother withdrew to a small dower house in the village. True to form, she even made him buy the deer – and when he asked me to resume the management of the park, I said I would love to, but that there was a problem.

'What's that?' he asked.

'It's just that I'm not on speaking terms with your mother.'

'That's all right,' he said. 'Neither am I.'

10

Glenfeshie

URING MY HISTORICAL researches I often came across the name
Glenfeshie, an estate high in the Cairngorms, which appears to
have been one of the earliest forests let for sport. The idea of a shooting lease was so novel in 1812 that when the owner, the Duke of
Gordon, placed advertisements in the newpapers, offering a sporting
lease, he was widely misunderstood. Most of the people who
answered supposed that the place was some sort of farm which had
been let go, but could be made productive again, and the duke's factor
was obliged to disabuse them. 'From what you state of yourself,' he
told one prospective tenant, 'I must be candid in mentioning that I do
not think the place will be suitable for you, as it has no House, is
remote and mountainous, and very inaccessible for want of roads.' A
gentleman from Scarborough received the same kind of answer: 'The
only sportsmen from your part of the Kingdom whom it might probably suit are such as could afford to preserve the land entirely for Deer

and Moorgame; and who, being in the prime of life, could encamp for a few weeks among the hills during the shooting season.'

In spite of the drawbacks, tenants were found, among them the Ellice family, who took the place in the 1830s, and shot what were, by today's standards, prodigious numbers of grouse. The bag in 1839, for instance, was 1816 brace – three times the highest amount recorded in recent years – and the huge total, all the more remarkable in that it was shot with muzzle-loading weapons, can have been achieved only through intensive predator-control. With no law to stop them, the gamekeepers killed every creature which they took to be an enemy: not just foxes, stoats, weasels and wild cats, but golden eagles, sea eagles, ospreys and kites, among many other species. And if the keepers were indiscriminate in their choice of targets, the sportsmen were even more so. One day in 1836 members of the Glenfeshie party, out after grouse, heard shots from high up the hill, where (the game-keeper reported) they found:

Mr Golding lying on the ground with his gun in a hole, in which he had discharged its contents, being in a state of great excitement. We learned from him that he had shot an eagle. Having descended into the hole, I succeeded in extricating the carcase, which to the surprise of all turned out to be a *horned sheep*.

In those days there were very few deer on the ground, and in most years the Ellices managed to shoot only three or four; an entry in their game book for 20th August 1839 records the 'immense excitement' triggered by a report that deer had been seen coming on to their preserve from the neighbouring forest of Gaick:

Ghillies, shepherds and dogs … started up the Feshie and found about fifty hinds and eight harts just crossing the burn to go home again. A well-drilled volley at 300 yards brought down the best beast of the lot.

Later, numbers steadily built up to the point at which Glenfeshie became one of the most celebrated deer forests in the Highlands, with the reputation of being a prime reservoir of stags. I got to know the estate during the 1970s through the kindness of the laird, Tony Dulverton, head of the Wills tobacco family. A tall, slim man, with a beaky face and a gruff manner that to some extent disguised his shyness, he was a mustard-keen forester who combined boundless enthusiasm for trees with a lifelong interest in deer. His twin passions were reflected in two of the many public posts he held: President of the British Deer Society and of the Timber Growers' Association. In the south he inherited a splendid estate – Batsford Park, near Moreton-in-Marsh, where he revived and expanded the arboretum created by Lord Redesdale, raising it to a level of national importance; and at Glenfeshie he not only put in over 1700 acres of new plantations, but also, by intelligent husbandry, greatly improved the standard of the deer.

The welfare of the deer was his prime concern. Knowing that they would destroy the trees if they gained access to them too early, he fenced the new plantations, his plan being to remove the barriers when the trees were big enough to survive. The new woods were created for the long-term benefit of the deer, and they were planted not in enormous blocks, like those of the Forestry Commission, but in relatively small stands, with gaps left open between them so that in harsh weather the deer could still come down to the low ground.

Glenfeshie is a spectacularly high forest, but its conformation is quite different from that of Knoydart. Instead of jagged peaks, much of the highest ground consists of a plateau at or above 3000 feet, marching with the Cairngorms Nature Reserve. The Feshie, running due north in a glen through the centre of the estate, is a tributary of the Spey, and the lodge, ten miles up the glen from the village of Kincraig, itself stands 1100 feet above sea-level. Aviemore, with its main road, ski-runs and intensive tourist activity, is close outside the northern boundary, but to the south the hills run away into Atholl territory, specifically Glen Bruar, beloved of William Scrope.

Tony was always a most generous host, and enjoyed taking friends to the hill, himself acting as stalker and leading the party. In matters of hill-craft and deer recognition, his skill matched that of any professional, and only the onset of slight deafness reduced his capability. One day, with the rut well advanced, he and I were making our way cautiously up a ridge when I heard, or rather felt, a deep roar that sounded as if it had come from amazingly close range. Another stag was roaring far up the hill above us, but this sound – more of a rumble than a roar – was *so* close that it seemed to vibrate through the ground, as if I had picked it up with my boots.

I leaned forward and tapped my guide on the shoulder. 'Look out,' I whispered. 'There's a stag somewhere very close to us.'

Tony dismissed my warning tersely. 'Rubbish!' he said. 'It's that fellow up there' – and he pointed to the skyline ahead. But when he took two more steps uphill and looked over a little rise, a dozen gleaming white antler points suddenly popped into view about ten yards ahead of us, and a stag heaved itself out of the peaty pool in which it had been wallowing. Away it went, coal black and dripping; and Tony, having scanned it quickly with his binoculars, muttered, 'Damned royal!' – a description which conveyed his irritation at the fact that the beast was too good to shoot, and that he had doubted my word, but also his pleasure at having such a fine animal on the forest.

Countless days on the hill had made him expert at assessing stags from a distance, and he was a first-class shot. His expertise with a rifle derived partly from the Second World War, when, as an officer in the Lovat Scouts, he formed a new sniper wing by collecting a group of stalkers and ghillies and harnessing their skills at rifle-shooting, fieldcraft, camouflage and spying with telescopes (itself a special art requiring much practice). The Army found that the hill-men's natural abilities formed an excellent basis for snipers' specialist training.

One of the many lessons I learnt from him was the necessity of well-conducted target practice. Not for him a casual blast-off at some spot on a rock and a cheerful 'Och, that's fine.' Nor would he let anyone fire at a conventional target with a black centre, on which it might not be possible to see where a bullet had struck. He insisted on making up his own targets with a patch of buff-coloured paper two inches square stuck on a white background, on which every bullet-hole was clearly visible, whether in the bull or the surround; and if you could not hit that two-inch patch at a range of 100 yards, you did not take the rifle to the hill. In fact the plateau at Glenfeshie, though very high, was so flat that shots often had to be taken at 200 yards, and we therefore practised at that range as well.

In the 1970s Tony bought a David Lloyd rifle – a marvellously accurate weapon, designed and built by a single, dedicated craftsman. For more than thirty years, at his home Pipewell Hall near Kettering in Northamptonshire, Lloyd worked on the development of a telescopic sight-mount so rigidly built into the action of the rifle that no amount of shocks could shift its setting. In the early days, when many mounts were frail and unreliable, *his* model was the exception, so strong that one could use the sight as a carrying-handle. A story was told of how a Land Rover turned over into a ravine and was written off among the rocks, but a David Lloyd rifle rescued from the wreck remained unscathed, with the sight still perfectly aligned. Another rifle – the one used by his own family – was zeroed in 1952 and was still shooting perfectly, without adjustment, forty years later.

An absolute perfectionist, Lloyd progressively refined his invention, and established his own test-range at Pipewell, where he or prospective customers could shoot through the window of a little hut, sitting comfortably in an armchair, at ranges up to 400 yards. He also developed a new calibre – the .244 magnum – for which the cartridges were necked-down .375 rounds. The result was a relatively small bullet with exceptionally high velocity, and the design was taken over by Holland & Holland. The combination of a very fast bullet and the patent sight made a David Lloyd a Rolls Royce of a weapon. The price – £5000 or more – was also in the top league, and there was a certain aristocratic arrogance about the rifle, in that it had no safety catch. This peculiarity derived from the fact that when Lloyd himself stalked at Glen Cassley, his own forest in Sutherland (where he shot over 2000 stags), he always had a man carry the rifle for him and hand it over just before he wanted to fire, so that (he maintained) a safety catch was unnecessary.

Armed with his .244, Tony Dulverton was a dead shot, very quick and decisive – and he needed to be, for a normal annual cull at Glenfeshie was 150 stags and 150 hinds, and he himself took a leading role in operations, especially towards the climax of the rut, when stags had to be got quickly before they lost too much condition. On one memorable day he sent three of us young men out, each with a stalker and a ghillie, and he went out on his own in what he called his 'tank' – a new type of all-terrain vehicle – driving it himself. He returned with two stags, and each of us got four – and fourteen in the day was regarded as a satisfactory bag.

As part of his deer management programme, he took to spreading basic slag (a form of fertiliser) on the flat ground beside the Feshie river – and this, combined with selective culling, brought about a striking improvement in the health of the herd: during the twenty years in which he ran the estate the average weight of stags went up by two stone, from 12.6 to 14.7, and the number of royals and ten-pointers increased dramatically. The area fertilised was small in relation to the whole (only ninety acres out of 45,000), but its bright green grass proved of incalculable benefit: in the evenings deer of all ages came pouring down on to it, and research showed that especially in winter a small amount of fresh food enabled them to digest rough herbage such as heather shoots, which was often all they could find elsewhere. That intake of good-quality nourishment saved hundreds of lives, for without it, in a harsh winter, many Highland deer die of starvation and hypothermia, unable to maintain their body temperature.

Sad to relate, this policy of slagging the flats put Tony at loggerheads with the Nature Conservancy Council (fore-runner of Scottish Natural Heritage), which maintained that fertilisation might change or damage the native flora. To him, this was a ridiculous idea, and he obtained strong support from the Red Deer Commission in his contention that the health of the deer was more important than that of a few obscure plants along the river. He also incurred the wrath of the Conservancy by putting in a gravel road right up onto the plateau, above 3000 feet, so that the carcases of shot deer could be extracted from that area. Tony was always liable to become forthright in argument, and as one senior official of the NCC put it, 'he gave us a very robust sense of his position'. In the end the disputes became so acrimonious that he lost patience and sold the forest – a miserable conclusion to twenty-one years of expenditure and effort.

Long before that happened, he and his wife Ruth showed outstanding generosity to me personally by twice letting me take over the entire estate for a fortnight in September. The stalking, the grouse-shooting, the fishing and the lodge (which had just been comprehensively refurbished, with a brand-new kitchen), together with the services of the stalkers and ghillies and their ponies and vehicles – everything was given free. Galvanised by this amazing offer, I summoned my usual squad of assassins, together with a couple of new recruits and two girls to run the house, and we had the holiday of our lives.

My instructions were to shoot as many stags as possible, and although during our first visit we managed to get twenty, we should have done better. There were an unaccountable number of misses (twelve, including two by me) – mostly the result, I think, of people being asked to take longer shots than they were used to. A rifleman who claims that he never misses is not worth serious consideration. Almost as bad is one who trots out specious excuses: 'The stalker put me off by talking too much' … 'The deer were about to take off'... 'The stag turned just as I fired' … 'The sun was in my eyes' … 'The midges were frightful.' The truth is that anyone can shake with an attack of stag fever or suffer a momentary lapse of concentration: the tiniest error is enough to make the bullet fly high, low or wide. Whenever some member of the party came back lamenting a miss, of course I sympathised and tried to help analyse what had gone wrong; but secretly I was rather glad, for it meant that the person in question had had a proper stalk, and that as a result of his or her lapse, we had an extra stag to get.

To make up for misses on the hill, we also got ten roe, which Tony greatly encouraged us to shoot, as they were damaging one of the young plantations. I can still see the revulsion on the face of our excellent cook, Lavinia Rome, as I came into the kitchen at the lodge with a handful of roe livers, which were dripping blood on to the floor. (Tony's neighbours in Gloucestershire were astonished and chagrined when he introduced some roe to Batsford, where of course they multiplied and caused havoc. Cotswold farmers do not share the romantic view of Spanish hunters, who call roe *el fantasma del bosce* – the ghost of the wood. Rather, they see them as a menace to farming and forestry, even though the Batsford estate culls eighty or more every year.)

The fishing at Glenfeshie was a disappointment. The river was low, and although we could see salmon in the deeper pools, no fly, spinner or worm could shift them. In the end, exasperated by our lack of success, I initiated a fish shoot, which involved almost all our party, including two senior executives of national companies – Simon Hornby, then Chairman of W.H. Smith, and David Lyon, Managing Director of Redland Tiles.

We concentrated our attack on one deep pool overhung by a rock, from which we could see straight down into the water. The salmon were there, all right, holding themselves steady against the current. After our first attempts with bows and arrows had proved futile, we resorted to heavier weapons in the form of deer rifles, and for half an hour blazed away at the fish with .270s and .243s, firing vertically down from a distance of no more than ten feet. At every shot a fountain of water rocketed skywards, hitting the firer in the face, but the fish remained, if not unmoved, absolutely unscathed. For some reason we simply could not hit them. Either we were aiming in the wrong place, our vision and telescopic sights confused by the refraction of the water, or else the impact on the surface was flattening and retarding the soft-nosed bullets to such an extent that they were not reaching the targets.

Simon had read somewhere that if one dumps foliage in a pool, fish will take shelter in it, and he kept ordering his servant Blondie (a former German prisoner of war) to throw in more heather. So Blondie was racing about, tearing up heather and flinging it into the water, and those not shooting were running up and down shouting contradictory instructions – until at last we managed to flush one salmon out through the narrow neck at the lower end of the pool, where we intercepted it in a net designed to catch deer calves for tagging, and borrowed from the Nature Conservancy. Our single victim weighed over 11 lbs, and we ate it ceremonially that evening; but of course news of our doings soon found its way south to the laird, who sent up a terse message telling us to stop harassing the fish.

The dour character of the river scarcely mattered, for the stalking was of the highest class. One slight drawback was the number of Munros (peaks of over 3000 feet) which the forest encompassed, and the fact that part of the ground lay within the Cairngorms National Park. The big hills attracted hikers and climbers like magnets, and although the estate put up notices at critical points, asking walkers not to use certain paths during the stalking season, and pointing out the dangers involved, some people always paid no attention them – though whether out of negligence or bloody-mindedness, no one could say.

One day the Head Stalker, Sandy Walker, and I spent some time working our way into the top of a vertiginously steep corrie known as 'The Bond Street'. Already I had had one alarming experience there, when I took a shot almost vertically down, over the edge of a very small platform, which itself was sloping so much that the stalker had to lie across the backs of my knees to make sure that I did not slide off into the abyss.

On this later day we could see stags lying low down on the opposite face, and we were debating how to approach them when a gaggle of eight or ten brightly anoraked hikers appeared, coming up the path in the bottom of the gorge several hundred feet below us. Since they had ignored the notice at the start of the path, I reckoned we were justified in giving them a fright, so I aimed the .300 magnum at a big stone beyond them, and let drive.

BOOM! In that rock-bound defile the noise was tremendous. Echoes rolled round the cliffs, thundering back from all directions, and of course the stags departed at high speed – but they would have gone anyway as they got the hikers' wind. The walkers stopped, and then cut about, darting this way and that as they looked up all round through binoculars. They had no chance of seeing us, for Sandy and I kept still, tucked in under a big stone on a very rough patch of hill, and they could not tell where the shot had come from. Through our binoculars we watched them get out their maps and hold a conference about what to do next. We hoped they would turn back, but to our irritation they carried on in the same direction. Later we heard that within a few minutes they met our pony-man, Jock, bringing down a stag which we had killed in the morning – and when they complained, saying they had nearly been shot, far from showing sympathy he instantly gave them a bollocking and told them to pay attention to warning signs in future.

As always, I revelled in the challenge of the highest ground, and the tremendous views it gave; but the glen itself was also gloriously attractive, and full of history. At the spot known as the Duchess of Bedford's, stubs of stone walls and the remains of a chimney buttress still mark the place where seven huts once stood in the little green plain. This was the camping ground of Georgiana, second wife of the sixth Duke of Bedford, a large and ebullient woman who had a holiday home in the form of the Doune, at Rothiemurchus, but who, according to Sir Walter Scott, had such 'a passion for the heather' that she moved up to the wilder and grander setting of Glenfeshie every autumn. She also had a passion for the painter Edwin Landseer, twenty years her junior, who painted her portrait several times and often stayed at Woburn, her palatial home in Bedfordshire.

Her husband was remarkably relaxed about this association, and although she refused the painter when he proposed to her, the family acknowledge that he was the father of at least two of her ten children.

Year after year she lured him to her encampment in the glen, where, beside the river, she had built a tiny village of huts made from wood and turf on stone foundations. The artist set up another cluster of primitive dwellings close by, and the accommodation in both was evidently basic, for in the estate game-book he wrote 'Glenfeshie Ballad No. 1':

> The boards so green were hung aroung with skins of
>   cats and foxes.
> All sat by day on wooden chairs and slept in wooden
>   boxes.
> Two slept together in one room, in huts which let no
>   cold in …

No matter that the buildings were ramshackle: Landseer set about decorating them with frescoes, and on the plaster above the fireplace in his own principal hut he painted a group of deer dominated by a suspicious hind. He also executed several sketches in Georgiana's central bothy, and in the hut she used as a dining room. Sad to relate, after the death of the Duchess in 1853 the buildings fell into disrepair, and by the time Queen Victoria came down the glen on her first grand peregrination in 1860, the encampment was so decrepit that most of the frescoes had been destroyed. Nevertheless, the Queen called the site 'the scene of Landseer's glory', and found it both attractive and melancholy. 'We were quite enchanted with the beauty of the view,' she wrote in her journal; but then her spirits were depressed by a meeting with Lord and Lady Alexander Russell, members of the Bedford family: 'They feel deeply the ruin of the place where they formerly lived, as it no longer belongs to them.'

A hundred and fifty years later, some of the Queen's sadness lingers on. The Duchess of Bedford's is still a lovely place, but the relics of her passionate involvement with Landseer and the Highlands are pathetically worn away.

Stalking at Glenfeshie was no small challenge, and we always hoped for a north wind, which would draw the stags to the north end of the forest, where they would be halted by a combination of fenced forestry and the skiing complex above Aviemore. When I asked one of the ghillies what would happen if the north wind blew for weeks on end, and the deer kept heading into it, he replied, 'Ach, it's no bother. The towerists drive them back!' On the other hand, a persistent south wind was a worry: if we disturbed deer anywhere near the march, it would draw them off our ground and away into the wilds of Bruar, whence they might not return for many days.

None of our party had any supernatural experience at Glenfeshie, but I listened eagerly to stories of strange happenings in the neighbouring forest of Gaick, where a giant fish called the Dorman was said to inhabit the loch, and where in 1800 the lodge was crushed by an avalanche which killed the four stalkers staying there. The more fanciful stories concerned Murdoch, an old stalker of about that date, who was out after hinds one morning when to his amazement he saw some tiny women dressed in green milking the deer. Later, on the Doune Hill behind the lodge, when he tried to shoot a hind, the animal kept changing into a woman and back into a deer, until he killed it, in animal form. At once he was overcome by drowsiness, but when he lay down in the heather, a voice roared out, 'Murdoch, Murdoch, you have this day slain the only maid of the Doune.'

The story sounds like a fairy tale, but it was corroborated in a strange way by a latter-day stalker, Colonel Jimmy Dennis, whom I knew. He too stalked at Gaick, and one afternoon, having shot a stag and sent the pony-boy off with it, he sat down to enjoy the view – whereupon he became aware of a slight disturbance near the head of a burn. Something small and rust-red was moving about on the grass round the spring, but every time he put his telescope on it, the object disappeared. By shading his brow, he made out that it was a diminutive creature of human shape, like a child in a pixie hood – yet when he moved towards it, again it vanished. At the time he said nothing to the other people in the lodge, fearing to make a fool of himself;

but when, years later in Glen Bruar, he mentioned the experience to his stalker, the man immediately answered, 'Then ye've seen the sprite of Gaick.'

On our last morning at Glenfeshie, before we left for the long drive south, I thought I would stretch my legs by walking straight up Carn Dearg Beag, the hill behind the lodge. Because the morning was fairly mild, and in any case I intended to keep moving, I wore no jacket or jersey – just a white T-shirt – and I took no precautions about keeping out of sight. Nevertheless, when I saw a large group of stags above me, I went through the motions of stalking them, and very soon came up behind an old dry-stone wall which ran along the contours. I was well within range – less than 100 yards from them – and had I been trying to shoot one, I am sure they would have been away like smoke. Yet when I stood up in full view, with my whole trunk above the wall, they took practically no notice. Somehow they divined that I was no threat – and when I recounted the incident to Tony Dulverton, he said scornfully, 'They probably thought you were a blasted sheep.'

Two years later, to our great delight, he and Ruth once again gave us the run of lodge and estate. I assembled a similar party, and this time we performed slightly better, getting twenty-four stags (with fewer misses) and forty-four grouse. Once more we failed to catch any salmon, but this time we did forbear from trying to shoot the fish.

11

Wormsley

S TONOR CONTINUED TO OCCUPY much of my spare time; but then yet another stalking opportunity arose a few miles further north, in the form of Wormsley, a wonderfully attractive estate of over 2000 acres, heavily wooded and well populated with fallow. Typical Chiltern country, its core is a broad central valley which runs north-and-south, with gently sloping fields cradled between beech-woods that crown the ridges on either side. Subsidiary valleys wind away into deeper forest on either hand, lending the whole area an air of surprise and secrecy. It was these woods which, in earlier days, provided the furniture-makers of High Wycombe with much of their raw material.

When I first knew the estate, it belonged to John Fane, whose family – connected with that of William Scrope – had owned it for nearly 250 years. They once kept a private pack of hounds known as 'Mr Fane's Harriers', and in 1840, aping the mock-medieval Eglinton Tournament held in Ayrshire a year earlier, they staged a tournament of their own, mounted on donkeys. Traces of medieval farmsteads can still be found in the the woods: mossy banks, flint foundations and clay rooftiles hint at the sites of former dwellings, now grown over by trees.

A shy and charming bachelor, John was one of the world's great procrastinators, always on the point of effecting improvements yet never quite managing to achieve them, and over the years he had allowed the place to fall into a state of astonishing dereliction. He himself lived alone in the fine, white Georgian house tucked in against a hill near the head of the main valley, but seventeen other estate houses stood empty, several of them on the verge of collapse, and the land was in a dreadful state.

It was as if the whole valley had been forgotten. The fields were scarcely cultivated, scrub had invaded the hill pastures, the hedges had run riot, most of the fences had disappeared, and everywhere in the woods fallen beech trees lay rotting – hundreds of tons of firewood going to waste. The kitchen garden, which had a sweet little cottage built into its surrounding brick wall, had long since gone wild, but was still a fruitful source of scrumped apples and pears in the autumn. The gravel roads were so deeply pot-holed that ordinary cars could scarcely negotiate them, especially in wet weather, when the huge hollows became lakes – and indeed one of John's ploys for ensnaring a young woman was to ask her to dinner, telling her she had better leave her car at the bottom gate, two miles away, rather than risk smashing it up. He would then collect his guest in a Land Rover, and when she wanted to leave, decline to take her. Altogether, the estate had an abandoned, almost medieval look, and it would have furnished a perfect setting for a film of a Hardy novel.

Of course the haphazard agriculture and minimal forestry made the place ideal for deer, and if the sheer extent of the woods rendered culling difficult, the lack of fences greatly facilitated movement from one field to another, and I had much memorable stalking. Often an early-morning start and a long patrol produced no result, but occasionally I had an astonishing burst of luck – as on the damp, murky day when, at first light, I crept down through a mature beech-wood to spy a young plantation on the opposite slope of the valley.

Out there among the brambles and young trees a dozen fallow does and fawns were feeding, and because the wind and poor light were in my favour, they did not see me as I settled myself into a solid firing position against the base of a trunk. This meant that I had time to choose my first target – an old-looking doe at the far side of the bunch – and pure chance dictated that as she tumbled at my shot, she keeled over into a heap of dry brushwood with a tremendous crash. This brought the rest of the deer hurtling downhill towards me. The instant they stopped, I knocked out another with a neck shot, and then two more as they bolted a few more yards and again suddenly pulled up, confused by echoes and uncertain where the danger lay. I had all four down in about thirty seconds, and although I had landed myself with the problem of extracting them from deep brambles, I at least had some compensation for all the blank mornings earlier that winter.

The entire estate was like one large game ranch, and some of the deer had grown old and cunning. One September evening, in an autumn of late harvest, I walked over the rim of a hill and down the edge of a wood, with a field of barley on my right. Presently I saw something sticking out of the crop about seventy yards below. Binoculars revealed the antlers of an aged buck, going back: definitely a cull beast. Quickly deciding to try and get him, I anchored my dog to a sapling and settled myself in a good firing position, planning to whistle him to his feet and shoot when he stood up.

I gave the loudest whistle I could manage. I could tell he'd heard it, because the antlers twitched round, back and round again, so that they came to rest facing in my direction – but still I could not see even the top of his head. I whistled again and clapped my hands. No movement. I began to declaim Shakespeare in a loud voice – 'Tomorrow and tomorrow and tomorrow'. The sole reaction was that the antlers went down even lower, so that only the tips were in view. I shouted. Nothing. I tried a line or two from the Hallelujah chorus: *For the Lord*

God is king, and reigneth … Hallelujah! Hallelujah! But Handel made no impression. I picked up a dead branch and beat on the fence so that the top wire twanged noisily. Still nothing.

I decided that the buck must be enmeshed in fence wire, like the stag we had found at Suisgill, with his hind legs bound to his neck so that he was hardly able to move. All the more reason, then, to put him out of his misery. The only possible tactic was to advance on him with rifle at the ready, and put a bullet into his head as soon as it came into view.

At that moment a heavy shower set in. Rain-drops hissed into the standing barley with such a racket that they obliterated the sounds of my approach as I started down. Now he was only forty yards away. Thirty. Twenty. Still I could see nothing but the upper half of his antlers. Fifteen yards. Already the shower was passing on. As its noise lessened, my footsteps were audibly crunching the corn stalks. Surely he must be hearing me?

Ten yards – and *whoosh!* In a flash he was on his feet and away like the blazes, clearing the barley in huge bounds, offering no chance of a shot. Far from being ill or disabled, he was in the most beautiful condition, his coat shining, his flanks rippling: he looked – as our gamekeeper would have put it – as right as ninepence. It was not wire, but his own accumulated guile, that had kept him down flat, chin on the ground, until the last possible moment.

In recent years a newcomer had infiltrated the Chilterns – the muntjac, or barking deer, an odd-shaped and (to my eye) rather ugly little creature, characterised by its jerky gait and pig-like attitude when walking, with its head held lower than the rest of its body, and by its habit, if surprised, of dashing away with its tail stuck straight up in the air above its back. The common name derives from the harsh, single barks which it gives when alarmed or defending territory: the staccato calls are often widely spaced at intervals of ten or more seconds, and may go on for fifteen or twenty minutes. Especially at night, the sound can be very disconcerting – and the first time it rang out in the valley where we live now, the sheep ran together into a tight flock and came rushing downhill for the shelter of the farmyard, clearly afraid that some dangerous predator was at large.

The ancestors of these exotic invaders from the Far East were imported by the eleventh Duke of Bedford, who released them into his park at Woburn in the early years of the twentieth century. Before long some escaped and spread out across Bedfordshire, but their diaspora was greatly accelerated by humans secretly catching a few and letting them loose in other counties.

Another factor (in my experience) is that muntjac prefer to live in small family groups rather than in herds, so that when any particular wood becomes over-populated, the younger animals are pushed out, and the result is a kind of rolling take-over of new territory. Not that the little deer never congregate: once, when we were rabbiting and a terrier went into a large patch of brambles, there was a startling explosion as no fewer than seven muntjac erupted with chattering barks. We could only suppose that a doe in season had attracted a crowd of suitors – and one reason for the species' rapid increase has been the unusual reproductive cycle of the females, which do not come into season annually, like other species of deer, but ovulate within a few days of giving birth.

In many areas muntjac do little harm, but they can annihilate desirable plants like bluebells, orchids and primroses, and frustrate efforts to restore coppiced woodlands by browsing off every new hazel shoot that appears. Nowhere has damage been more regrettable than in Monks Wood, a national nature reserve in Essex, where for years English Nature refused to allow any culling, on the grounds that it might upset members of the public. Only after the organisation had spent fortunes on futile electric fences did the authorities agree that planned culls were the only way of saving the wood from total ruin.

Barking deer are also a menace in gardens: they can slip in through the smallest gap in a fence, and their appetite for roses and runner beans is prodigious. I have known many a lady conservationist turn vicious when she finds her border savagely pruned: one in particular used to ring me up whenever she saw deer approaching her territory and call for their immediate extermination. As to means of protection: at one time lion dung was reckoned a sovereign remedy for repelling deer, but that seems to have gone out of fashion, as has a bag of human hair, and even the foul-smelling compound Renardine has little effect.

Culling muntjac is difficult, for the creatures tend to frequent thick woodland, and seem to be constantly on the move, poking about in the undergrowth, showing themselves only now and then. Luckily German stalkers will pay to shoot them, since the animal does not exist elsewhere in Europe: to any *Jäger* it is a novelty, and accommodating, in that it can best be tackled from a high seat. Although I saw muntjac almost every day at Wormsley, I made no special effort to pursue them, because I was always keener to increase my cull of fallow, and did not want to disturb the woods with shots that would produce only a small return.

John Fane's great weakness – inherited, I suspect, in his genes – was for the horses. He generally owned a racehorse, or part of one, and lost much of what money he had in betting. Whenever I built up a bit of a fund from sales of venison, he liked to have it in cash, and I would take him a brown envelope containing a few hundred pounds, which I knew would trickle away like water. Considering the state his property was in, he always seemed remarkably cheerful, and he was incurably optimistic, always about to repair one or other of the decaying houses.

Although commendably reluctant to dispose of any asset, he did sell one outlying farmhouse, and this was done up to the nines by people from London, who came to it at weekends. It stood in a small valley of its own, cut off from the main part of the estate, and when I approached the site one morning, I got quite some shock. I was with a German friend, Dicky Michel, a keen stalker, and as we walked round a ridge I explained to him that in a moment we would be straight above the only house which had been refurbished. Seconds later we came over the rise and looked down – and to my amazement, the house had vanished. For a moment I thought my sense of direction had gone, and that I was looking into the wrong valley. Dicky assumed I had been pulling his leg. But then, through binoculars, we discerned a pile of ash and the twisted remains of a building: in the owners' absence, the house had burned to the ground.

In the end, the inevitable happened: John ran out of money, and was forced to sell. He retained a small house just outside the estate, but went to live mainly in London, where he found the attitude of the inhabitants rather strange. He told a friend that a woman rushed out of her house in Chelsea and shouted at him as he was walking past with his Labrador.

'What happened?' asked the friend. 'Had your dog gone into her garden for a leak?'

'No,' said John indignantly. 'But I had.'

Luckily Wormsley was bought on behalf of the billionaire philanthropist J. Paul Getty II, who, with the advice of the London art dealer Christopher Gibbs and others, restored and enhanced the property with great skill, imagination and sympathy. The Georgian house was renovated from top to bottom, and a new library, designed to house Getty's collection of rare books, was built on to the back of it, dominated by a circular, flint-faced tower, reminiscent of the Round Tower in Windsor Castle.

The decaying farmhouses and cottages were re-built and modernised, with bathrooms and central heating; the eighteenth-century barns, with their weather-boarded walls and tiled roofs, were reconstructed; eight miles of private road were re-surfaced to the highest standards; a deer park was formed by enclosing an area beside the main house, and a lake was created with water from a borehole sunk hundreds of feet into the chalk. New fences were built, the old hedges tamed, the woods cleared of rotting timber, and thousands of new trees planted. It was here that there took place the first secret release of red kites, imported from Spain and Sweden, at the start of a re-introduction programme which has proved enormously successful.

John Fane revealed his magnanimous nature when invited back to
shoot by the new owner. Far from showing any sign of jealousy or
resentment at the transformation which had been wrought on his old
property, he was enthusiastic about every improvement he saw. 'What
a wonderful job they've made of the stables!' he exclaimed. 'And those
barns – marvellous!'

Later, Getty gratified his passion for cricket by having a field laid
out, complete with rustic pavilion, a short distance down the valley
from the house. Like all the other works, this was carried out by professionals, and after one false start, when the square persistently
flooded, there emerged a most beautiful playing surface, not just with
a first-class pitch, but with an outfield whose turf rivalled the perfection of the sward at Lord's. Every national team came for a match
when it was touring – Australians, South Africans, West Indians, Sri
Lankans – and one sight never to be forgotten was that of the great
Brian Lara straight-driving a six over the sight-screen while a kite
flapped lazily across the outfield in front of the scorers' hut. Yet whenever a crowd gathered for one of Getty's private matches, I guarantee
I was the only person present who had witnessed a scene that had
taken place on this very field in its earlier guise, when, during the rut,
two weary fallow bucks squared up for battle, but after a token push
at each other, decided that they were already too exhausted to fight
any more, and staggered away side by side like a couple of old gentlemen repairing to their club.

It was no surprise to me that the deer survived Wormsley's change
of ownership as well as anybody. The new park was stocked initially
by the simple expedient of leaving leaps open, so that fallow jumped
in from outside. These pioneers were reinforced by consignments of
red deer from the parks at Melbury and Windsor; but any number of
fallow were left outside the enclosure, and the woods are full of their
descendants to this day.

12

Strathossian

MY SPORTING LIFE HAS been much influenced by contact with the Fleming family, starting from the time when my godfather Peter Fleming – elder brother of Ian, creator of James Bond – gave me the run of his estate. It was Peter's grandfather Robert who made the first of the family's fortunes: a financial genius, he left school in Dundee at fourteen, and later founded the family bank, Robert Fleming, which became immensely successful. His elder son, Valentine (Peter's father), was killed in the First World War, and during the 1930s, because Peter appeared to have been disinherited, his uncle Phil gave him the 2000-acre Nettlebed Estate. When Peter's youngest brother Michael died of wounds during the Second World War, his widow, Tish, brought her family to live in Nettlebed, so that I grew up with another Valentine (my exact contemporary), his brothers Christopher and David, and his sister Gillie.

In the 1970s Peter's second brother, Richard, began taking a month's lease of Strathossian, a relatively small forest near Spean

Bridge, east of Fort William; and because he himself wanted to stalk for only part of that time, in several successive seasons he kindly sub-let one or two weeks to me, at a very modest rate. The low rental was due partly to his generosity, but more to the fact that the only house available was a tiny, early Victorian bothy, primitive to a degree.

A little white building, with a barn and cowshed alongside, it stood in splendid isolation, backed by a small fir plantation, in the middle of a great sweep of empty moorland. Our first sight of it was never to be forgotten. As we approached on the gravel road, driving up through Forestry Commission plantations from the hamlet of Fersit, we came round one more bend, and suddenly there it was, miles ahead and below, a mere dot in the heart of the wilderness.

That first, romantic view of the place was the best, for on closer inspection its deficiencies were revealed all too clearly. The main room was the kitchen, with a bare concrete floor, and part of its space had been closed off with a wooden partition to form a bathroom. A Rayburn solid-fuel stove did heat the room and the water tolerably well, if sufficiently razzed up, but there was no electricity, and dim yellow light came from gas-lamps set in the ceilings, which were blackened with soot. Next to the kitchen a little square, pine-boarded sitting-room was similarly lit, and furnished with two or three battered arm-chairs. On the other side of the kitchen was a bedroom, and upstairs three more tiny bedrooms were crammed in under the angles of the roof; no sheets were provided, and the blankets were filthy beyond description. Altogether, the house was wretchedly uncomfortable – a sharp come-down after the sybaritic delights of the lodge at Glenfeshie – but its limitations were somehow so ridiculous that we instantly fell in love with it, and returned year after year.

One of its eccentricities was the fact that whenever there was frost at night – a frequent ocurrence in late autumn – the pipe bringing water overland from the burn froze solid; another, that the only drinking vessels were superannuated jam jars of numerous different shapes, sizes and vintages. This last quirk was due to the fact that Richard, like all Flemings, was frugal to a degree, and saw no point in importing expensive glasses which might get broken. Whisky, he maintained, tasted just the same when drunk from pots once full of marmalade or chutney as it did from Waterford crystal.

Strathossian's topography needs a word of explanation. The ground had been part of Corrour, the much larger forest marching with it to the west. During the 1890s Corrour's owner, Sir John Stirling-Maxwell, built a lodge at the eastern end of Loch Ossian, but the site he chose was dauntingly remote. At first the only means of access to it was a pony path leading up Strathossian; but then the railway companies planned to put a line through the forest, and Sir John granted them permission on two conditions: one, that they built a halt, with a platform, at which his guests might leave or board the train, and two, that they guaranteed to keep the station open for as long as his family owned the estate. The railway went past four miles west of his new lodge, and to save his guests a long and uncomfortable drive by horse carriage, he installed the yacht *Cailleach* on Loch Ossian, so that they could cover three quarters of the distance by water. For another eighty years that combination of rail and private road was the only way into Corrour; but then the Forestry Commission put in the gravel track which now sweeps round in a big curve above the Strathossian bothy, so that people could drive in from the north.

Our little lodge could be made very cosy by roaring up the Rayburn to a dangerous heat and lighting the fire in the sitting-room, and we were content to live in some squalor; but the number of people in the party had to be kept small, and four or five was the practical limit. In two of our years David Lyon and I were the only men, nobly supported by Phylla, who did the cooking. One year we were joined by Gerry, and once we invited the distinguished potter Alan Caiger-Smith, who came with his wife Anne-Marie. She, too, was an excellent cook, and did not flinch at the lodge's shortcomings.

The greatest asset on the forest was the stalker, Geordie Nairn, an exceptionally nice and amusing companion on the hill, always full of ideas and enthusiasm, and extraordinarily skilful at marshalling his stags. He lived in the hamlet of Fersit, not far from the north end of the ground, and, besides acting as stalker on the open hill, was responsible for culling deer in the plantations which the Forestry Commission had established on the north part of Corrour Estate.

Almost all our stalking took place on a single massif, Carn Dearg, bounded in the west by the ten-mile stretch of Loch Treig, with the railway line running above the shore, and in the east by the River Ossian, which separated the forest from neighbouring Ardverikie. In summer our hill, which had half a dozen separate summits, harboured a mighty herd of stags – maybe 500 of them; and in early September Geordie's aim was always the same – to nip one stag here, another there, by sniping round the edges and taking every care not to disturb the main lot. If we pushed them too hard, they might break out prematurely, and charge away across the river into Ardverikie, where unscrupulous trophy-hunters would have a chance to shoot the royals and ten-pointers that we had been carefully sparing. Geordie knew that when the rut started in earnest towards the end of the month the stags would break out anyway, but he was always determined to delay the exodus for as long as possible – and in this he was amazingly clever.

One day, however, we took a shot too far, and suddenly the entire army of stags was on the move, heading eastwards towards the river at breakneck speed. It was a magnificent sight – several hundred animals flowing downhill in a tawny torrent – but the last thing we had hoped to see, and we too raced downhill, risking broken ankles and yelling like fiends, parallel with the leaders of the avalanche, firing our rifles across their bows. For a couple of minutes it looked as though all was lost; but then, miraculously, the front-runners faltered and stopped. A few more shots finally turned them, and back they went up the hill.

Another indispensable member of our entourage was Alec Stewart, from North Uist, the senior ghillie, who with his crimson wattles and beaky nose looked more like a cock grouse than any other human I have seen. Every morning he went through a hilarious pantomime of trying to catch Billy, the white Garron pony. Although the house boasted a pony park (or paddock) of sorts, its fence had long since collapsed, and there was no way of keeping a loose horse within bounds. Billy knew this, of course, and so played hard to get. Only his weakness for strawberry-jam sandwiches made him vulnerable. Every morning Alec would creep towards him, proferring the juiciest item from his piece in one hand, and concealing a halter behind his back with the other. On some days Billy would allow himself to be collared, but on others, as Alec put it, he would 'give you the heels' and set off at full gallop, snorting, for Corrour, three miles away.

On days when we were stalking on the eastern side of our massif, Alec and the pony would follow us up, and, if we got a stag, they would take it down to the nearest point on the road. There Alec, who had an ungovernable passion for decapitation, would immediately hack off its head and park it beside the body – a gruesome sight for any stranger who happened to come past.

Operations on the western side of the massif were more problematical, for the face which ran the whole length of Loch Treig was too steep for a horse, and the only way of extracting a beast from that side was to drag it down to the railway. Geordie had a long-standing agreement with the crew of what he called 'the speeder' – the flat little maintenance wagon that went south along the line every morning, and returned in the afternoon – whereby if they saw a body lying beside the track, they would load it up and throw it off at Tulloch, the next station along the line. From our point of view, the snag was that the speeder went home at about 3.30 pm, so that if we wanted to make use of it, we had to have our stag beside the line before that. On the other hand, we gained from the fact that Geordie usually rewarded the railwaymen with a stag, and sometimes, when we had shot our own allocation, he would say, 'Christ – I'm needing one for the railway', and off we would go after another.

He also made singular use of the track for his own purposes. From somewhere he had acquired a four-wheeled bogie, and he had fitted it up with the pedals, crank and chain from a bicycle, which he connected to a sprocket on one of the axles. Also on board was an arm-chair, in which he could recline in comfort while pedalling. Late at night he would launch this contraption on to the main railway line at Corrour and pedal gently down the gradient northwards, sweeping the hill on his right with a powerful spotlight, and letting drive with his rifle at any fox which the beam picked up. Because there was so little disturbance down there, the foxes were fairly naïve, and he scored heavily; but if ever an extra, unannounced train had come down the line, he would have been in dire trouble. He could, I suppose, have jumped clear, but his beloved foxing bogie would have been annihilated.

For the stalkers, ghillies and other estate employees at Corrour, the railway offered the only chance of going out for a drink in the evening. By boarding the last down train, they could trundle for ten or twelve minutes to the next stop, Rannoch, and lower a pint or a dram before catching the last train back. Luckily the windows of the bar commanded a view of the line, so that when they saw the engine labouring up the gradient towards them, they had a few moments in which to drain their glasses before dashing for the platform.

Stalking with Geordie was always highly entertaining – although every day it involved some punishing climbs. 'I think we'll go up a bit' was his most frequent refrain, and again and again we re-learnt the painful lesson that the ridge above you, which looks like the summit, is not the summit at all, but merely a ledge on the way up. Sometimes, in contrast, we had to go almost vertically downwards – as on a day when we spotted stags lying on a little plateau below us. Leaving David in charge of my young Labrador Pumpkin (so called because as a puppy she had been as nearly spherical as made no difference), Geordie and I wormed our way over the edge of the hill and began sliding feet first, on our backs, down a precipitous grass slope. It was a thrilling stalk, because we were in full view of the stags, and any sudden movement might have put them away.

Our objective was to reach a small gully which ran along the contour, directly across our front, perhaps a hundred yards below us, and maybe a hundred and fifty yards from the nearest stag. If we could gain that shallow channel, it would give us a tiny bit of cover, and its far bank would make a good point off which to fire.

Down we went, easing ourselves forward inches at a time, digging the heels of our boots into the short turf to stop ourselves sliding faster, with frequent pauses. All went well, and in due course we reached the gully, where we found that, as we had hoped, we were half-hidden from most of the stags. But then, before I had had time to swivel round into a firing position, there came a sudden, slithering rush from behind, and a second later I had a huge, warm, black bolster thrashing madly round the back of my neck. Pumpkin had burst her moorings above, hurtled down the grass face and flung herself on me, all four feet in the air, electrified by delight at catching up.

So much for our own painstaking approach! Geordie was uttering fearful imprecations under his breath, but by some miracle the deer had not noticed the dog's whirlwind descent. They were all still lying peacefully, and I reached round to grab her by the scruff of her neck, drag her down into the channel and suppress her while Geordie carried out a quick appraisal. Then, having chosen a stag and pointed it out, he assumed control of the dog while I took the shot.

Besides being tactically expert, he was an ace at roaring – a skill of high value during the rut. By cupping his hands either side of his mouth, he could produce a roar convincing enough to stop most stags in their tracks, or even bring them towards him, and this lured many a beast to its doom, especially in the forestry plantations, where the deer were extremely hard to see.

Alan Caiger-Smith, an artist and a gentle soul, had never done any stalking; rather, he came for the wild country, of which he drew fine, bold sketches. One day, however, we persuaded him that he should be the Rifle, and after he had taken a couple of accurate shots at a target, we set off with Geordie on what turned out to be a marathon walk. Several potentially exciting operations were foiled by the fickle wind, or by hinds popping up unexpectedly, and at 4 pm we sat down temporarily exhausted on a heathery knoll. To wind Alan up, I said to

Geordie, 'We'd better break it to him, that in this forest, if we haven't got anything by four o'clock, we go on the double.'

'Aye,' replied Geordie, quick as a flash, 'and at six o'clock we sprint.'

For a moment Alan looked fit to die – but then a miracle occurred. All day we had searched in vain for a shootable stag, and now, as we sat there, down the hill towards us came a single beast, walking slowly. A quick scrutiny confirmed that it was old and decrepit: its antlers were thin, its brow-points short, its coat staring – an ideal animal to cull. Without moving another step, Alan lay down and shot it expertly – and when we got it to the roadside, Alec lost not a moment before he whipped its head off.

One year the lodge at Strathossian was not available: incredible as it sounded, improvements were being made to the sewer. We had our usual area over which to stalk, but for accommodation we were obliged to resort to a building at Corrour. There the main lodge had twice been burnt to the ground – the site being so remote that no help could arrive in time to save it – and the existing lodge was a wooden Colt structure; but we were assigned to the old, cold, damp and depressing Corrie Creagach House, which entirely lacked the charm of Strathossian.

It so happened that David had brought with him Lillis, an American not yet familiar with the barbarities of life in the Highlands, and we were dismayed to find that we had confronted her with a freezing bedroom, a primitive bathroom and a horrible little kitchen. We need not have worried: she rose to the challenge with unquenchable resilience and good humour, and at one point, when we asked our supporters to supper, she cooked such a potent brew of carrots with garlic that it made one of the ghillies' hair stand on end.

Among our party that year was a boyfriend of our daughter Alice, young Bill Russell, who came up from London on the overnight train. At 7 am I drove down to the station to meet him, and spent a few minutes revelling in the isolation of that lonely outpost. Hygiene, I could see, was not the preoccupation of the station mistress. The door of her house stood open, and a steady traffic of ducks, geese and sheep paddled in and out on a carpet of semi-liquid mud. The surroundings, on the other hand, were pristine. Everywhere in the heather cock grouse were sounding off like alarm clocks – *go-back, go-back, go-back* – but apart from that, the silence was perfect, and the frosty air tasted gloriously clean.

Presently the rails began to give off a faint twanging sound, and the long, sleek train came squealing in. A few weary-looking hikers staggered off, but no Bill. 'Damn!' I thought as the train pulled away to the north. 'He missed it – and because we had no telephone, he couldn't let us know.' Back at the lodge without him, I had breakfast, and we all went to the hill. Not until late that afternoon did we discover what had happened. He *had* been on the train, but towards the back, and when he looked out of the window as it came to the halt, all he could see was miles of heather stretching away on either side of the line. He therefore concluded that the train was pausing to let another pass, in the middle of nowhere, and sat tight.

Too late, he realised his mistake: the train was already picking up speed when he saw the station building, and he was carried on up Loch Treig-side to Tulloch. There he jumped off, and eventually he found some tradesman who was going to Corrour and gave him a lift; but by the time he arrived, we had disappeared into the wilds, and he missed the day's stalking, except that he managed to join us just as we were starting back. That evening he was so exhausted – not having slept on the train – that he fell asleep in the middle of an impromptu ceilidh. This was no mean feat, for we had persuaded Alec to bring his pipes, and he squalled out many favourites, among them *Mairi's Wedding*, which he consented to play only when he had been assured that David and Lillis were about to get married. The noise in the small, low-ceilinged room was shattering, but Bill was oblivious to it: inch by inch he sank down on the floor, with his head propped against the wall, and drifted off to sleep almost underneath the piper's chair.

By the terms of our lease, David and I were allowed to shoot roe and black game, and one year, when we had the lodge to ourselves, we brought no meat with us, aiming to live off the land. We managed very well, and sometimes had a roe carcase hanging on the back of one of the bedroom doors. I skinned and plucked, and he cooked with great skill, so that we ate like kings. Gargantuan breakfasts became our speciality: we were taking so much exercise that after a while we found it necessary, after porridge, eggs, bacon and toast, to down a pint of Brakspear's bitter before we went to the hill.

We also had the right – indeed, we were invited – to shoot any stags we could find in the plantation along the north side of Loch Ossian, where the deer were knocking the young trees about. One evening at dusk, spying across the loch with telescopes from the opposite shore, we spotted a truly immense stag, a real monster, emerge from the conifers and start grazing on one of the wide rides that ran along the contour between the trees. Soon he was joined by another beast, less spectacular, but also with a big body.

It was too late to set up a stalk that evening, but we were back on the scene at first light, and decided on a slow walk-through, into the wind, with David on the middle ride, myself below. I had gone about half-way along the wood when I saw Pumpkin start to lift her nose high, in the attitude that unmistakably meant 'Deer'. I stopped and watched her. Higher and higher went her nose. A gentle wind was coming down to us out of the trees. Keeping still, but facing straight into the breeze, I suddenly realised that between two small spruce I could see the back and flank of a deer, no more than twenty yards away. From the size of the bit in view, I knew it was a stag, and in my excitement I jumped to the conclusion that it must be the monster.

Normally, I would not have fired through a screen of small branches; but because of the slope the background was perfectly safe, and the range was so short that I reckoned that the bullet would not deviate much, even if it hit a twig. So, with infinitely slow movements, I un-shouldered my rifle, brought it up on to my long stick, aimed where I judged the beast's heart must be, and pulled the trigger. At the shot the thicket erupted, and the stag charged off uphill. Seconds later there came a tremendous crash as it went down, followed by sundry thrashing noises, and I knew it was dead.

My God, I thought: what incredible luck! I've got the monster. For quite a long time, perhaps a minute, I stood still, winding down from the excitement. Then I took a step forward – and the movement provoked another explosion, even more violent than the first. Out went a second stag, tearing through the trees like a thunderbolt, and as it crossed a gap I saw at once that *this* was the monster. It had been standing within ten yards of me, and after the shot its native cunning had held it rooted to the spot until it knew for sure where I was. My mind flashed back to the fallow buck which had kept its head down in the barley at Wormsley: here was another illustration of the survival of the craftiest. It turned out that the stag I had shot was a hefty beast and weighed sixteen stone; but he was only the side-kick, and the big fellow must have turned twenty stone at least.

Where do ideas come from? Sometimes the only answer to the question seems to be 'From nowhere' – and that was so when I suddenly got the notion of an action novel set in the Highlands. At the time I was labouring to finish a factual book about the training of Royal Air Force fast-jet pilots, which was to accompany a television series. In the early stages of the project I had had some exhilarating flights in Phantoms, Buccaneers and Hawk trainers, but the completion of the text had become rather tedious, and I was longing to finish it. Then one night I unaccountably woke up in the early hours with a fully fledged plot in my head.

A man is on the run in the western Highlands. A former member of Special Forces, he suffered a severe head injury during his service, and in consequence is mentally unbalanced. He has conceived a passionate hatred of the Forestry Commission because its plantations, planted and fenced without thought for the deer, cut the animals off from the low ground and so cause huge mortality in winter. He starts setting fire to plantations, and because it is September, stalkers and ghillies join the police in hunting him. Then he accidentally kills a couple of elderly American tourists who have parked their caravan among the trees, so that now he is wanted for murder...

I felt some sympathy for my protagonist. At that date – the early 1980s – the Forestry Commission had a poor reputation, and I myself had seen the cruelty of their Highland planting programmes, in the form of bleached deer skeletons scattered along the topmost forest fences. The organisation was immensely bureaucratic and slow to react – as I discovered in the south, when I wrote asking urgently for permission to cull in a particular wood, because deer were emerging from it to devastate a crop of winter wheat. I sent off my letter early in January, and received a curt refusal during the second week of July.

Now, spurred on by slight personal animosity, I found it easy to develop the plot, especially as I could fit the action into country that I knew. I began the story with the fire-raiser sitting on the side of a hill I called Ben Allan, but in fact I was thinking of a point where I had shot a stag with Geordie high above Loch Treig. From there I had no difficulty in moving him erratically towards the west, until in the end, making for the coast and hoping to escape by boat, he is driven up Sgurr-na-Ciche and surrounded on the summit, leaving him no option but to jump.

The thriller came out under the title *Fire Falcon*. Reviews were encouraging, and a film producer, Chris Chrisafis, who quite by chance read one of the notices as he was passing through Zurich, bought an option on the movie rights. Soon he commissioned a script, and decreed that he, the scriptwriter Dave Humphries and I should make a reconnaissance trip to the Highlands to prospect for possible locations. Being a bit of a movie moghul, he set up the expedition in style, arranging for a helicopter to meet us at Glasgow airport, and also a Range Rover and driver, in case the weather was too bad to fly.

Whom should we find stranded at Glasgow but Robin Fleming, patriarch of the clan, and laird of Black Mount, the largest of the family's estates. He was on his way there, but something had gone wrong with his transport arrangements, and there was no one to meet him. When Chris magnanimously offered him a lift in the waiting helicopter, he was delighted to accept, and thirty minutes later we touched down on the grass in front of his lodge, cutting a tedious hour off his journey.

By then, however, bad weather was closing in. The clouds were down on the high tops, and although it was relatively calm in the glen, at high altitude a westerly gale was raging. Our pilot reluctantly announced that if we climbed into that wind, we would probably land in Norway; so we decided to abandon ideas of exploring by air that day, and to carry on in the Range Rover, which was following up behind.

To fill in time while we waited, the pilot sportingly offered to take a party on a joy-ride above the A9 and down through Glencoe. First aboard was Hamish Menzies, Head Stalker at Black Mount, who was so broad in the beam that when he eased himself down into the centre of the rear seat, he only just fitted between the arm-rests, and one of the watching ghillies made the immortal remark, 'I'm thinking if Hamish rises, the helicopter will rise with him.'

Rise with him it did – though not in the fashion the ghillie had intended – and we had a thrilling flight through the pass, with the glistening ramparts of Buchaille Etive Mor and the other bastions disappearing into the mist above us, and the earth-bound traffic crawling below. After a sweep round above Ballachulish, we flitted back up the glen, and by the time we reached Black Mount again, our car, driven by a glamorous, long-legged blonde, was there to pick us up.

I was particularly anxious for Chris to see something of Knoydart, as I hoped that the grandeur of the landscape would fire him up; but first we made for Strathossian, which I thought would appeal to him because of its isolation. As we bounced up the rough track through the forestry plantations he began to grow restive, not liking the dense masses of conifers, and saying irritably, 'Are you sure we want to come here?'

'Hang on,' I told him. 'You'll see what I mean in a moment.'

Then, as we came round the bend that opened up the view, and saw the little white house marooned in its sea of wilderness, he suddenly became electrified with enthusiasm 'Jesus!' he cried. 'Look at that!' (as if I hadn't seen it). 'This is fantastic!' – and at once he and Dave began, as it were, competing for use of the lodge. 'This has got to be the place where our man holes up ... No, no – this is Billy's house.'

We spent that night in one of the hotels on the shore of Loch Linnhe, on the outskirts of Fort William. The next morning was fine, and Chris summoned the helicopter to pick us up at 9 am. In it swept to land on the forecourt, and away went most of the hotel's potted plants, blasted down the lochside by the downdraft from the rotor. Luckily the proprietor was so pleased with the publicity generated by the spectacular arrival and departure that he cheerfully waved his plants goodbye.

On that brilliant morning Knoydart looked magnificent. The burns were boiling white, and the great rock faces were still gleaming from the night's rain. Now for the first time I saw the summit of Sgurr-na-Ciche from all angles, and when we went wheeling up close to the cliffs above the Carnach river, I felt exhilarated, on level terms with the eagles. Chris, however, did not like it, and called over the intercom, 'Let's get out of here' – so we went down and landed briefly on a beach on the north shore of Loch Morar, where we worked out possible action sequences.

From there we cut back to have another look at Strathossian, landing beside Geordie Nairn's house at Fersit. 'Travelling in style, now!' he said jovially as he came out to greet us. Hanging on a fence was a set of enormous antlers, which still had streaks of fresh blood about the skull plate – evidently a recent cull. From the size of the head, I could tell that the beast must have been living in the plantations, rather than on the open hill – and as woodland stags are notoriously secretive and hard to find, I asked, 'How did you get him?'

'Oh,' said Geordie, 'I roared him up, no bother.'

'And how far away was he when you shot him?'

'Right on the end of my barrel!'

Once again Chris was looking uncomfortable, so we took off

again, to make a pass over Strathossian lodge and straight up the hill behind it. In a few seconds we skimmed up that steep face, which took us half an hour to climb on foot, and I again enjoyed a brief sensation of bird-like freedom; but after a while I decided that this was an unsatisfactory menthod of travel, for although it was fast, and gave one fantastic views, it cut one off from all the sounds and smells of the environment.

Alas, the film was never made. The script was re-written and re-written, becoming more and more violent, until it bore little relation to the original story, and the elusive combination of the right actor, the right director and the right amount of money never materialised. So our airborne reconnaissance was wasted, but it had been a wonderful adventure while it lasted.

13

Glenkinglass

ONE SUMMER WE AGAIN renewed our connection with the Fleming family when we stayed for a week at Glenetive Lodge, where Robin had replaced an old lodge with a brand-new one. I never knew the old building, from which (as the stalker Jock Fraser put it) 'you could see the damp running out the door to meet you', but the new lodge was compact and extremely comfortable.

It stood near the end of the single-track road that winds south-wards for thirteen miles down a dramatically steep glen from a point on the main highway, the A9, just east of Glencoe. On almost every day of our visit tourists not well versed in map-reading drove past the lodge confident in the belief that they were heading for Oban, only to find that the tarmac came to an abrupt end in the water of Loch Etive. Shocked, and usually enraged, they came and asked how far they had to go, and what was their best route – whereupon I told them. 'It's seventy-six miles, and in that direction,' pointing back the way they had come.

With us were an old friend, Archie Eglinton, his wife Marian and their young boys. Our stay began with a minor disaster, in that the wine which I had ordered in the south had not arrived. We were eager to have some white wine to go with all the fish we were going to catch, so in desperation I rang the nearest emporium, the general store at Tyndrum, which stocked what the lady called 'the Piesporter', and another white, La Vie de France. The Piesporter turned out just about drinkable, but La Vie de France was a horror – Jeyes fluid tinctured with diesel oil, or possibly vice versa – and we poured the only bottle we opened down the sink.

A much greater disaster almost ensued. One night young William, who was going through a tiresome phase, kept waking his mother up with various excuses. When he did it for the fourth time, saying 'I can smell burning,' Marian reluctantly got up to investigate. It was just as well she did, for the Aga cooker had caught fire.

All adult members of the party rapidly assembled in the narrow kitchen, which contained a great deal of smart new woodwork. Flames were belching out of the oil-fired cooker, front and top, even though the oven doors were closed and the hotplate covers were down. The wooden cupboard doors, on the other side of the kitchen about four feet from the front of the stove, were already too hot to touch.

Obviously the first essential was to turn off the oil supply – but how? At that date none of us had any experience of Agas, and no idea what to do. Feverish consultation of a manual, found in a drawer, directed us to a switch on the fuel pump, round the right-hand end of the stove; but when I lifted the little lever, as directed, it apparently had no effect. I tried several times – up, down, up down. The movement seeemed indeterminate, and because the fire was roaring, I could not hear whether or not the lever was clicking, as it should be. Later I learnt that I had done the right thing, and that it takes time for the oil already in or past the pump to be burnt off; but in the fierce heat of the moment this was not apparent, and as I crouched on the floor in my pyjamas, with flames still spurting, I kept thinking, 'If this thing blows, we'll all be fished out of Loch Etive in little pieces – but at least we won't know anything about it.'

Thank heaven, it did not blow. Gradually the fire subsided; we all went back to bed, and William was exonerated from the charge of deliberately vexatious behaviour. In the morning, to our chagrin, we learnt that the Aga had been serviced by a professional engineer only a couple of days before, and that the man had made some frightful mistake in putting it back together.

The Etive is an excellent spate river, which fishes beautifully after rain; but the water falls quickly, and one has to catch it at the right moment. Archie – a human otter, of great piscatory cunning and wide experience – caught several good fish during the week, as we expected he would; but one morning I, a beginner, amazed him (and myself) by landing two salmon, of 8 lbs and 5 lbs, within five minutes. Of course I returned again and again to that same pool, but never so much as shifted another.

In spite of the frustrations, we thoroughly enjoyed our stay, which included an eight-hour foray after ptarmigan round the top of the 3000 foot hill known as the Highlander; and one evening was greatly enlivened by a party at Dalness, the next Fleming stronghold up-river. The best part of it, for us, was the way Robin held the singing together by pumping out bass rhythms on his accordion, but at the same time generously allowing our daughter Alice, who was then in her teens and had a smaller accordion, to lead the tunes.

Half-way down Loch Etive a magnificent glen runs away into the mountains to the east. We had looked into it when fishing on the loch, and its steep, wild character had immediately attracted me. There was one little white house at Ardmaddy, on the estuary of the river, but otherwise no sign of habitation. Inquiries revealed that Glenkinglass had once been part of the huge Black Mount forest, and that now it belonged to Major John Schuster and his wife Lorna, whose mother, Dorothy Wyfold, had been a daughter of Robert Fleming, founder of the family bank. It seemed that when the family bought Black Mount in the 1920s, the Wyfolds had put up some of the money and had taken Glenkinglass as their share. Here, then, was yet another Fleming connection, and yet another good-natured laird, who agreed to let us a fortnight of stalking in the next season.

We had already stayed in plenty of remote lodges, but the warning order sent out by the Schusters' factor was enough to set my pulse racing. The letter explained that after leaving the main road two miles beyond the western end of Loch Awe, one had to drive up a Forestry Commission track that ended in a small car-park beside an old railway wagon. Thereafter, things grew tougher. Anyone with a low-slung or heavily loaded car was advised to leave it in the park and transfer to an estate Land Rover, for the track beyond was marked on the map only as a footpath, and was exceedingly rough. Even vehicles which managed to reach the estuary of the Kinglass river would not be able to drive up the glen to the lodge, for there was only a footbridge over the mouth of the stream, and all luggage had to be carried across and loaded into an estate 4x4 on the other side.

When we tackled the approach in August, the first stretch beyond the car park seemed not too bad, but after a little farmstead called Glennoe, the next section became diabolical. The road – if you could call it that – had recently been cut out of the hillside: it wound steeply up, down, in and out, and its surface consisted of mud, loose stones and rounded boulders big enough to gralloch any vehicle. Progress along it was extremely slow, and made nerve-racking by the frequent crunching impacts beneath our feet; but eventually we arrived at the river, where we transhipped our baggage and went on up the glen by Land Rover.

If this road, also, was awful, the scenery was stunning. The river was down below us on the right, and the hills on either side looked formidably steep and large. The texture of the landscape was quite different from that of Knoydart or Glenfeshie: here the slopes and faces seemed smoother and more grassy. The whole glen had an open, expansive and immensely attractive look.

At last, seven miles from the lochside and two-and-a-half hours from the main road, we reached our destination – a small lodge standing on level ground only a few yards from the river bank. A typical Victorian outpost, which once would have been occupied by parties who had walked out from Black Mount, it was plainly built, with dark wood boarding inside, and few frills. Yet it was more spacious than it looked, with five bedrooms and two bathrooms. Its most awkward feature was the kitchen / dining room in which, when the table was set for eight, there was very little space for the cook – our daughter Alice, then seventeen – to manoeuvre.

As a base for operations, it was perfect: there was no communication with, or interference from, the outside world; majestic hills rose all round; we could start stalking from the front door, and fishermen were within one cast of the river bank. Besides, the lodge contained a priceless exhibit: the pair of miniature brass dumb-bells, bound with green leather, which Lady Wyfold was wont to whirl round her head every morning outside the front door, to strengthen her wrists for casting.

Our sole link with civilisation was the resident stalker, Tim Healy, who had a telephone in his house at Ardmaddy on the lochside, and could bring messages when he came up in the morning, or take them down in the evening. A most unusual character to find on the hill, he was (and is) not a Scot at all, but a sassenach from Dorset, who was working in graphic design in Poole when he went up to Aviemore for a winter holiday. 'And that,' as he said, 'was it'.

Ever since he could remember he had harboured a dream of living in mountains, with trees and water around, and as a boy he had been constantly on the moors behind his home. Once he had seen Aviemore and the Cairngorms, his fate was sealed. He went back to London for a year, but then at the age of twenty hit out for the north with his guitar and a fishing rod. For six months he lived rough, travelling over the hills and sleeping in empty houses, of which he found any number in Shetland: before the oil boom, many of the inhabitants had abandoned their homesteads and departed, leaving their furniture and even their cutlery in place. 'The young people had gone,' he remembered, 'and when the old people died, there was nobody to replace them.' A chance meeting with a forester from the Balmoral estate led to various jobs as a grouse-beater, and then as a stalking ghillie at Invercauld, before he came to Glenkinglass, first as a ghillie and then as the stalker, in about 1975.

A small man, dark and wiry, he learnt his new trade as thoroughly as any Highlander, and by the time we met him he had acquired an impressive knowledge of the hill and the deer. Luckily he and I hit it off from the start, but I soon saw that he was not a man to suffer fools; if he met one, he would walk him for hours in places where he knew no stags would be found, and at least once he had ordered a visitor off the hill for failing to obey instructions.

Among his foibles was a firm belief in the Wee Folk – the fairy dwellers in the glen – which he had picked up from members of the Wyfold family, and in particular from Pet Herman-Hodge, who claimed to have heard the little people singing around the ruin of the dry-stone building known as the Old School, which stood beside the glen road at Narrachan on the way down to Ardmaddy. That certainly seemed to be the centre of strange activities, and Tim's conviction was strengthened by the fact that hikers who camped in the ruin often told him, without being asked, that they had heard the sound of bells at night, and mysterious voices singing.

In any case, no amount of ribbing from us would shake his belief that it paid to humour the Wee Folk. Every time we crossed the Acharn bridge over the river on our way to the hill, he would hide sweets in a cavity beneath a big stone on a mound, and, sceptical though we were, we could not deny that when we returned that way in the evening, the sweets had gone. Maybe otters had got them, maybe some wandering hiker – but who could say?

One sceptic was big Sandy Robbins, the second stalker. When he first came to the glen, Tim showed him the cavity, and put sweets into it while he was watching. When they came back in the evening, to find that the offering had disappeared, Sandy was first shocked, but then accused Tim of having snatched the sweets away by sleight of hand while pretending to leave them – which he had not done.

Sandy was young, large and fit, a cheerful and amusing leader, but he moved at a fearful speed – far too fast – and one member of our party after another came back at dusk exhausted by his death marches. Alice and I had a desperately long day with him: we never got near a stag, and walked (we reckoned) twenty-two miles. After about fifteen miles Pumpkin staged a lie-down strike – a protest not easily dealt with, as she weighed about seventy pounds and anyway did not like being picked up. Fortunately, after a drink from a burn and the crusts of a sandwich left over from one of our pieces, she recovered and trotted on none the worse.

The sheer size of the country meant that all stalking days were long and arduous: inevitably we started from low in the glen or even lower on the lochside, and climbed to dizzying heights, but almost always we were rewarded by grand encounters with deer and the most magnificent views. One memorably fine, hot day Tim led myself and Gerry to the summit of Ben Cruachan, the five-peaked massif at the southern end of the forest. He knew there would be no deer up there, but just wanted us to revel in the surroundings; and as we sat in the sun on the main ridge, at about 3000 feet, he described how a tunnel big enough to admit vehicles had been bored through the bowels of the mountain beneath us, as part of the hydro-electric power station in an immense cavern way below us on Loch Awe-side.

Glenkinglass ground then extended to 50,000 acres, and encompassed no fewer than nine Munros, so that the ground was often disturbed by hikers and climbers – and never more annoyingly than on a day when Tim and I made a particularly distant expedition to the north, where a large group of stags had been seen lying on the lower flanks of the pyramid-topped Ben Starav. After nearly three hours of steady climbing we spotted the stags where we hoped they would be, and we were just planning our approach when down the steep slope beyond them an apparition came flying – a middle-aged or even elderly man wearing a red woollen hat with a bobble on top, running in a most ridiculous attitude, with both arms held high in front of him and splayed hands sawing at the air above his head, as if he were trying to show off and attract attention. He was not on any footpath, and he was heading straight for the deer, but, short of putting a shot across his bows, which would have scattered the stags anyway, there was nothing we could do to stop or divert him. On he came, over a crest, into full view of the deer, and away they went. Where *he* went, we could not tell, for somehow he vanished into the landscape, and we never saw him again; but our plan was ruined, and all we could do was head for home.

A luckier day was the one on which we took out a young friend, Luke Valner, in search of his first stag. For several hours things looked grim, as the clouds came down, blindfolding us, and there was nothing we could do except sit around and wait. But in the afternoon the mist suddenly cleared and after an exciting stalk Luke got his stag; then, as we started to pull it down, he hung back, brought out a small camera and took what turned out to be a magnificent photograph of Phylla, Pumpkin, the stag, myself and Tim poised against a stunning backdrop, which included a huge expanse of hill and about four miles of Loch Etive, fifteen hundred feet below, stretching away into the far distance. He later sent me a blown-up copy of the picture, about two feet by three, which I had framed and hung above the mantelpiece in my study, where it has remained ever since.

The fisher-people in our party needed to be patient, for the river rose and fell quickly, and if we got no rain for several days running, even the wiliest of them, Christopher (Puds) Royden, could make little impression on the salmon and sea-trout. When his teenage sons John and Richard took to the water in frustration, things were different, for he had taught them to tail fish, and it was by no means unusual for one of them to surface from a deep lie holding a salmon in either hand.

When conditions were right, the river's named pools – Double Dykes, Acharn, Ford, Narrachan Rock, Maiden and others – all became very exciting. One evening Tim took me to the Narrachan Long Run as dusk was falling. After heavy rain earlier in the day, the river was still full, but the water level was dropping, and he pronounced it to be ideal. 'Mend the line,' he urged after every cast, as I brought the fly back across the surface. 'Mend the line.' Again and again we moved a few steps downstream – and then suddenly there it was: a thrilling, deep judder on the line. I gave some exclamation and struck, whipping my rod tip upwards, but I was too slow to react. The fish had gone.

'Never mind,' said Tim. 'I've got to leave you now, but you'll get one in a moment.'

As he disappeared into the twilight, I carried on trying to cast as he had taught me, and the next half hour was pure magic. The sky was still full of ragged clouds, but the light was dying, and in the distance on both sides of the glen the peaks and ridges stood out in sharp black silhouette along the skyline. The surface of the river was alive with movement as the hurrying dark water rolled and swirled, gurgling with richness and urgency. Every sense told me that it must be *boiling* with fish on the move upstream.

Sure enough – all at once it came again: that thick, shuddering wriggle, heavier than the first pull. This time I struck faster, and the fish was on. Exactly how I got it into my landing-net, I cannot remember, but within a few minutes I had it on the bank – a 10-lb cock salmon. For me – very much an amateur angler – it was a moment never to be forgotten; and ever since I have cursed myself for not continuing to cast. Had I done so, I would surely have caught another and another in that perfect water – but I was already late for supper, and I knew people would be waiting for me in the lodge; so I picked up my prize and headed back through the dark.

By far the most memorable event of our second stay at Glenkinglass happened at the start of the visit. We arrived on Sunday afternoon, after the usual agonising grind along the lochside, the transfer of luggage and the drive up the glen. Tim told us that there had been little rain during the past few weeks, and the river looked depressingly low.

At the lodge we unpacked and settled ourselves in, and then

decided to stretch our legs by walking up the steep hill opposite.
Together with our son Guy, who was then sixteen, Phylla and I set off
up the left-hand side of the Raven Burn, which came down in a deep
ravine directly towards the house. After a while Phylla decided that we
were going too fast for her liking, so she sat on a rock while Guy and
I carried on up the hill. We had climbed several hundred yards when
she heard a faint shout. Looking up, she saw that we were walking
shoulder-to-shoulder, and she thought it odd that one of us should
have called out when we were so close together; but then, hearing
nothing else, she made her way down and back to the lodge. Guy and
I went on climbing until we reached a point at which the burn was
easy to cross: there we scrambled through it and came back down the
hill on the other side.

On Monday morning the weather was still dry. Tim drove up from
Ardmaddy as usual and took a stalking party to the hill above the area
round which we had walked. He was disappointed to find no deer up
there, and in jest blamed Guy and me for clearing the ground –
although in fact he knew we could not have done so, as we had gone
only a short distance from the lodge, and the wind had been in our
faces.

During the afternoon stormclouds began massing to the north-
west, and by tea-time, to the delight of the fishermen, rain had set in.
At 7 pm or so, as we were having a drink in the sitting-room, somebody suddenly said, 'God – look at that!' The window gave a fine view
of the Raven Burn, and we could see great jets of white spurting
out of its rocky channel. Clearly, there had been a cloudburst on the
high ground above, and immense quantities of water were suddenly
coming down. The lower part of the channel was still dry, but every
few seconds a fresh burst of white showed what rapid progress the
flood was making, as, one after another, stretches of the burn ex-
ploded into life. It was a mesmerising sight, and we raised our gin-
and-tonics to it, happy in the knowledge that the river was about to be
revitalised. What we could not know was that in the raging flood a
man was fighting for his life.

On Tuesday morning the river was in spate, and roaring as it passed the house. The fishers eyed it eagerly and prepared for a big day. Tim arrived promptly at nine, and we were again getting ready for the hill when first I and then another of the party heard a high call which we thought was a sheep. The noise of the river made it hard to tell where the sound had come from, but when I told Tim about it, and we listened again, he at once said, 'That isn't a sheep. It's a person.'

The cry seemed to have come from across the river, and when we looked up, we spotted something red moving a few yards to the right of the burn, maybe a thousand feet above us. Binoculars revealed a man lying on the hill and waving a red shirt or sweater. At once Tim took off towards him, accompanied by Ali Loder, a teenager who that summer was working on the forest as a ghillie. Through our glasses we watched them reach the man, and seconds later a red distress flare soared out, so another posse took off with an emergency kit of stretcher, ropes and blankets.

Twenty minutes later, gasping from the climb, we reached the casualty, and found a man who had broken his left thigh high up, almost at the hip. He was wearing nothing but a shirt, jersey and underpants; every inch of his bare legs was inflamed with midge-bites, and his thigh had turned nearly black around the injury. He was grey in the face, shuddering violently and intermittently speechless with pain.

The moment I saw him, I decided he was too badly hurt for us to take him down that rough, precipitous face. 'We need a cas-evac helicopter,' I said, and Tim went racing back down the mountain, to drive like the wind for Ardmaddy, and summon a rescue aircraft by telephone.

Up on the hillside we got the injured man into a dry jersey and wrapped him in blankets. Eased by a pain-killing tablet, he told us his story – and we quickly realised that we were witnessing the closing stages of an epic feat of will-power and endurance.

He was a Dutch maths teacher called Ton (short for Antonius) Peters, with short, reddish hair and beard, and he spoke perfect

English. Thirty-two years old, a marathon runner and experienced long-distance hiker, he had been on a solitary trek that would have taken him from Glasgow to Glencoe. He had no fears about travelling the wilderness on his own: he was used to solitary camping, and had told no one what he was doing. He had made good progress until the afternoon of the Friday, but then, at about 3.30 pm, he tried to cross the Raven Burn, slipped, and fell thirty feet into the ravine.

He knew at once that he was in trouble, for although shock had temporarily anaesthetised him, he could see the broken end of his left thigh bone pushing out against the muscles just below his hip. Many people would have panicked, but he kept his head. 'I thought of what an animal does when it's injured,' he said. 'For the first couple of days it lies up, gaining strength, and then gradually it gets moving again. I hoped I could do the same. I thought that after a couple of days the bone would start to knit, and I would be able to climb out of the gully.'

He had fallen into a pool, but he dragged himself out of the water and set up a makeshift camp on a slab of rock at the base of two water-falls – and there he spent the next four nights and three days. Lying on his back on a camping mattress, with his sleeping bag and tent spread over him, he was relatively comfortable. He had plenty of cereal to eat, and brewed up soup, savoury rice and tea on his gas cooker. An occasional aspirin helped dull the pain in his leg and enabled him to sleep for short periods, but he kept the four pain-killing tablets which he was carrying against the ordeal of trying to climb out of the ravine.

Whenever he thought he heard a sound that could have been made by humans, he shouted for help – and it must have been one of these calls that Phylla had heard on the Sunday afternoon. It was sheer bad luck he did not yell again a few minutes later, as Guy and I must have passed close by him on our way up, and then again on our way down.

After a while, he told us, he had begun to suffer mild hallucinations, and thought he could hear his mother talking. To pass the time he kept a diary, writing neatly in a notebook. Saturday and Sunday were mercifully dry, but on Monday afternoon (as we knew) it had begun to rain, gently at first, then harder – and at 7.20 the surge of white water which we had seen from the lodge had come roaring down the channel.

Peters's camp was destroyed. His equipment went first – tent, sleeping bag, mattress and pack were swept away. Then he himself was lifted bodily and flung down the ravine. How far he went, neither he nor we could determine, but it was at least 150 yards and over several waterfalls. As he was whirled over and over he could feel the ends of his broken bone grinding together, and when at last he fetched up doubled over a fallen tree, he knew he had to get out of the torrent, or he would drown.

By a superhuman effort he clawed his way up an almost vertical fifteen-foot rock face, and then up a steep bank of grass and heather. It took him nearly four hours to reach the lip of the ravine, and the ground he crossed was scrabbled black, as if a badger or fox had been caught in a snare. From his new position he could see straight down to our lodge, but even as he watched, to his dismay the lights went out as our generator shut down, and he was left to spend his fourth night in the open, now clad only in sodden shirt, jersey and underpants. Almost the worst part of his ordeal came in the morning, when, with daylight, midges swarmed out of the heather and settled in hundreds on his legs.

He recounted all this as we waited for the helicopter, and he seemed amazingly cheerful, worried only by the possibility that he might not be able to run again. A search of the ravine lower down yielded his pack and sleeping bag, both badly damaged, and while a couple of people went down to the lodge for a thermos of hot, sweet tea, Gerry, with his army training, laid out our haversacks and jackets in an H as a beacon for a rescue pilot. We reckoned we were in for a long wait: it would take Tim at least three-quarters of an hour to reach the telephone, and we didn't know how quickly a helicopter could be scrambled, or where it might come from. Luckily the sun shone and a breeze got up, putting the midges into cover.

At last we heard it – the thudding clatter of a heavy chopper – and there it was, a Sea King skimming over the ridges, not banana yellow, as I had expected, but drab green. The pilot evidently wanted to check his position, for he went down and landed beside the lodge and sat there for a few moments with his rotor still turning, as another of the crew jumped out to get directions. Just as he was putting on power to take off again, a small, white terrier took an aggressive rush at the machine, only to be blown backwards, head over heels, by the down-draught from its rotor.

A few seconds later the Sea King was overhead. Away went Gerry's carefully constructed H of marker bags and coats, scattered far down the hill; but that hardly mattered, as the crew had no trouble seeing us. The slope was far too steep for a landing, so the pilot hovered while a civilian doctor and two crewmen came down on the winches; then he pulled away over the glen, where he flew up and down in big sweeps until the patient was ready for collection. On the heather, the doctor checked Peters all over, gave him a sedative and sheathed both his legs in a pneumatic splint which held them tight together, before calling the aircraft back in. Then they lifted him gently onto a stretcher, and with the helicopter screaming overhead, only twenty feet above us, up he went on the winch, beaming and waving to anyone he could see. By 3.30 we were back in the lodge, with all thoughts of stalking abandoned, but fired up with memories of an extraordinary day.

We heard later that the surgeon who operated on Peters in Glasgow did such a skilled repair that his fears of being left permanently lame were dispelled, and he was able to run marathons again. He wrote me a letter of heart-felt gratitude, and for several years we maintained a friendly correspondence.

If he was unlucky to suffer the accident at all, he was incredibly fortunate to have it where he did, for the lodge at Glenkinglass was the only inhabited building within a seven-mile radius of the point at which he fell. Had he broken his leg in any deserted glen, and lost all his kit in a flash flood, the odds were that he would have died of exposure, and nothing would have been found of him but his bones.

Of all the friends who came with us to Glenkinglass, none was noisier or more stimulating than Max Hastings, who had recently distinguished himself by his front-line reports from the Falklands War. He did not altogether care for our stalking expeditions, which he found rather energetic, and he once claimed that I made him fire at a stag while lying flat on his back. But on the river he came into his own, and fished with enormous skill and zeal, his enjoyment clouded only by the fact that the deadline for completion of his book about the war was rapidly approaching.

It was this that made him leave on Saturday, instead of staying until Sunday, and after smoking out the company with a final cigar over breakfast in the crowded kitchen, he disappeared down the glen. We heard no more of him on Sunday, but then on Monday morning Tim came up with a message saying that Mr Hastings had left his wallet behind, and could we please look for it in his bedroom? The wallet, Max had told Tim on the telephone, was a specially expensive one given him by the *Daily Express* in recognition of his sterling work in the Falklands, and it contained all his credit cards, as well as a good deal of cash.

His small, square, bare bedroom had already been assigned to a successor, but a quick search confirmed that the wallet was not there, and this news went down to him that night. On Tuesday morning Tim brought another request: Mr Hastings had to admit that, as he went down the glen, the Maiden Pool had looked so inviting that he had felt obliged to give it a cast or two. Maybe he had dropped the wallet there? Could we please search round the Maiden Pool? This we did with ill grace, for the pool was surrounded by grass and bracken, and the wallet could have been anywhere in the undergrowth. Finding nothing, we sent down another negative report.

Come Wednesday, the message had changed again. Mr Hastings remembered that there was a gap behind the big log-box in the porch. Could we have a look there? There was indeed a gap about an inch, wide enough for a wallet to slip down; but in order to have a proper look, we had to empty the box and undo a couple of bolts before dragging it away from the wall. Nothing – and the message which Tim conveyed that evening was a little terse.

Silence fell, and I heard no more until three months later, when I got a card from Max, apologising profusely and saying that the wallet had got stuck in the lining of an anorak, where it had been reposing ever since.

Losing things seemed to be an occupational hazard at Glenkinglass. One year, as we were packing up to leave on Sunday morning, Gerry announced that he had could not find the keys of his car, which he had left in the Forestry Commission park, before the start of the bad road. After increasingly frantic searches through his clothes and equipment had failed to discover them, we told him his only option was to come with us and make sure he had not left them in the car.

There stood the dark-green Scirocco, firmly locked. From the Awe filling station on the main road he summoned up an AA mechanic, who managed to open the doors without damaging them, but was defeated by the ingenuity of the steering lock. Even though he took off the steering wheel and stripped the column down to a stump, that was all he could manage, and we were obliged to abandon Gerry to his fate – which was to spend the night in his sleeping bag on the floor of the filling station, until he could summon superior forces on Monday morning. As in the saga of Max and the wallet, a long delay intervened before the *dénouement*: it turned out that all the time the keys had been tucked away in the breast pocket of a filthy shirt which he had rolled up and stuffed into a kit-bag.

14

Lochaber

OFTEN AS WE DROVE UP the shore of Loch Linnhe towards Fort
William we looked across the water to our left, into the glorious array of mountains that ran back into the blue distance on the
other side. When I discovered that the estate was called Conaglen, and
that the stalking was for let, I recklessly booked a fortnight. I say 'recklessly', because by our modest standards the cost was astronomical –
and when we arrived there, we saw why.

The three-storey Victorian lodge was far larger than any of the
others in which we had stayed. No beauty, but notably spacious
and comfortable, it became even more agreeable when the owners,
John and Faith Guthrie, gave it an extensive and very expensive refit,
putting on a new roof, installing more than eighty double-glazed
windows, rearranging the bedrooms so that every one had its own
bathroom, and adding a walk-in refrigerator room next to the kitchen.
As Faith said, she was worried that they might transform the lodge
into a hotel rather than a house, but they and their architect skilfully

avoided that pit-fall, and made the place, with its full-size billiard table, ping-pong room fashioned from the old chapel, and four-hole golf course, an ideal base for a large party on holiday.

The lodge stands at the head of four acres of immaculate lawn, which slope gently down to a field generally occupied by Highland cattle. Beyond the field lies Loch Linnhe, and beyond that forested hills go up from the water's edge – a lovely prospect. Beside the house are elaborate flower and vegetable gardens, beautifully maintained, but immediately behind the lodge and its wooded policies the hills rise steep and bare, so that domestic and wild scenery are closely juxta-posed – a conjunction finely described by a former owner of the estate, Michael Mason, in his book *The Golden Evening*.

With the property came two stalkers, several ghillies, a fishing manager, a housekeeper-cook, two maids and a full-time gardener, to say nothing of stalking over 35,000 acres and fishing in two small rivers. We took a liking to the place at once, and became so fond of it that we returned six or seven times, encouraged by the genial support of the Guthries, who lived in Yorkshire.

The stalking ground is by any standards spectacular. Conaglen itself runs westwards for thirteen miles between towering ridges before ending in an amphitheatre of steep faces; and even beyond them the rocky heights of Sgurr Ptarmachan still belong to the estate. Sometimes we began operations right from the back of the lodge, climbing the Stalkers' Path that goes up through trees beside a burn before leading out onto the open hill. On other days we drove up the glen road – a rough gravel track – and took to the heights from some other start-point; but to tackle the western extremities of the ground we would go by road round three sides of a rectangle – nearly an hour's drive – up the shore of Loch Linnhe, left-handed round the corner of the land opposite Fort William, along the south shore of Loch Eil almost to Glenfinnan, and left again down a Forestry Commission track beside Loch Shiel to a place called Scamodale, where a single cottage stood near the foot of a great natural bowl scooped out of the hillside. From there a stiff climb brought us out onto ridges that commanded glorious views, on clear days as far as Orkney.

As in other forests, the core of our party was always made up of members of the family – my brothers-in-law Gerry Barstow and Alexander Lindsay, reinforced by wives and children. My niece Katy Stewart-Smith, a brilliant shot and an extremely chic stalker, often to be seen on the hill in a tweed suit with a skirt of positively Victorian length, soon justified her reputation as a born huntress, and her brother Christy was equally keen. He spoke for many when, in a thank-you letter, he enthused about the 'constantly surprising contrasts' that stalking throws up: 'Stalking quick, stalking slow, stalking cunning, stalking bold or ducking and diving while a light, uncertain breeze swirls menacingly.' Katy, in her stalking diary, was particularly deft at recording the minor absurdities of expeditions on the hill:

> The most entertaining moment of the day came when we stopped to sit down on some rocks for a breather. When we arose there was a wafer-thin addition to Anthony's behind. A small frog snoozing on a rock had mistaken his speedily descending behind for a cloud shadow and had not taken evasive action fast enough.
> Derek (the stalker): 'Och, yer sat on a puir wee froggie.'
> Anthony (peeling same off left cheek in confusion): 'Dear, oh dear!'

Most of our people had stalked before, but some had not, and in spite of my regular warnings a few arrived with totally inadequate boots or shoes. When one newcomer announced that he would bring his old army boots, I advised him to re-equip, but he would have none of it. His boots, he insisted, were the best in the world. In fact they gave him such poor support that after one day of slipping and sliding on the hill he was almost crippled by strains and blisters, and on Day Two he drove into Fort William to buy a new pair. Over the years we sent so many customers to Nevisport, the excellent emporium at the end of the High Street, that I felt the shop ought to offer us a discount.

In both our first two years the head stalker was Andy Aitken, a most agreeable fellow, and more considerate than many, in that on the hill he never forced the pace. Nevertheless, it was with him that I suffered a serious setback.

Having driven some five miles up the main glen, he, I and my nephew Christy left the Land Rover and worked our way up to the right into a high, narrow corrie known as the Slochd that cut through the main range of hills towards the north. From the moment we started climbing, I felt slightly off-colour, and I found the going unusually hard – but I put the trouble down to having had one dram too many the night before.

Presently we made contact with a large, scattered group of deer, mainly hinds, but with a shootable stag among them. They were restless – not because they had seen us, but because the rut was starting – and they kept grazing on ahead of us along the left-hand face of the corrie, drawn by the wind blowing through the gully from the north. The hillside was very uneven, dotted with large boulders and patches of bracken, and when we eventually managed to manoeuvre within range of the stag, we were in one of those patches of tall vegetation which made aiming awkward: the target was some way above us, and I had to raise the rifle as high as I could on my elbows to clear the fronds of bracken, so that I was far from steady.

At the shot the stag fell like a stone and rolled a few yards down the hill towards us. I knew straight away that although I had aimed at its shoulder, by a lucky chance I had hit it in the neck. No matter – it was dead, and its entourage had made off in a hurry, so I let loose Pansy, my latest Labrador, and sent her up the hill. In a few seconds we saw her find the stag, but instead of seizing it by the throat and shaking it about, as she normally did, she gave it no more than a cursory lick and carried on up the slope before disappearing.

We climbed to the stag, bled it, gralloched it and tied ropes to its feet and head. By then we had crossed the watershed, and were looking out to the north, towards Loch Eil: this meant that we could not drag the beast back the way we had come, and our only option was to take it down to the end of the road which came up from the other side through the big plantation at Duisky. Pansy had still not reported for duty – most unlike her – and as we were about to start dragging I had a sudden intuition. 'Hang on a minute,' I said. 'I'm just going to make sure we haven't shot something else as well.'

No more than fifteen yards further up the hill I looked over a ledge, and there was the bitch, sitting faithfully beside a dead hind. By an extraordinary fluke my bullet had gone through the stag's neck, and fragments of it had carried on in a kind of vertical spray. One piece had hit the hind in the forehead, another had knocked out her two central teeth, and a third had punctured her neck over the Adam's apple. It was clear that she had been killed instantly. We could hardly blame ourselves for not having seen her when I took the shot, since she had been lying in deep bracken – but of course Andy was upset that we had killed a beast out of season.

Now we had two carcases to drag. Luckily there was not far to go, and the route was all downhill. Andy and Christy managed the stag, while I took the hind, and at the corner of the forestry fence we pulled them up on to a smooth little knoll. We were then faced with a three-mile trek, back through the Slochd to the Land Rover. But we had gone only a few yards when I suddenly found that my strength had evaporated and I could hardly walk.

'Andy,' I said. 'I'm not going to make it.'

'What's the matter?'

'I don't know. I can't breathe.'

'Oh God!' He looked dreadfully worried and asked, 'Have you had a pain in your chest?'

'No – nothing. I'm just knackered.'

'Well – you'd better stay here while we go back for the vehicle. We'll come round and pick you up.'

With that the two set off, walking fast. I watched them disappear over the sky-line, then tottered a few steps into the plantation and lay down on my back on the gravel road. With my jacket wrapped tight round me, I was neither cold nor worried. On the contrary, I felt curiously calm – not frightened by the possibility that I had had a heart attack, but just accepting whatever had happened. I lay there for an hour and a half without discomfort, but I was glad when I heard the Land Rover bumping and scrunching up the track, and I hauled myself into it gratefully. Back in the lodge, I was so debilitated that I had to climb the stairs one at a time, resting on every step. I went to the hill no more that week, and in the south a specialist diagnosed my problem as arrhythmia, or irregular heart-beat, which luckily could be kept under control by medication.

Recovered, I described the two-with-one-shot episode in one of my weekly articles for the *Independent*. I said that we, the humans, had not done very well, in that we should have spotted the hind lying beyond the stag, and that the only person who came out of the encounter with full marks was Pansy. But for her (I wrote) we would have left £60 worth of venison lying on the hill.

This was too much for a reader somewhere in the north. In a furious letter to the editor, she condemned my article in rousing terms. Duff Hart-Davis must be sacked at once, she thundered. She had sent a complaint to the Press Council. She had cancelled her subscription to the paper. She had warned her next-door neighbours never to let their eight-year-old son see a copy of the *Independent* again. The entire article was a disgrace. As for my final remark about the dog – that was the most disgusting sentence she had ever read. In reply, I suggested that if she did not like reading about events that actually took place in the country, she might do well to switch to the *Guardian*.

When Andy moved on, he was succeeded as Head Stalker by Donald Kennedy, tall and fast-moving, a brilliant rifle-shot and highly knowledgeable about the hill, who became so engrossed in his approach to deer that he sometimes grew annoyed with slow, incompetent amateur riflemen, and gave them a piece of his mind. Occasionally, also, his attitude to female stalkers became less than chivalrous: one day Peggy, a visiting American (the wife of Lillis Lyon's cousin Louis) returned to the lodge in triumph, having shot her first stag, but exclaiming in amazement, 'Donald made me lie down in a place where so MANY stags had been to the bathroom!' Another time, a girl called Anna turned out wearing trousers of a rather hard material, which made a scraping noise as each leg passed the other. The air was absolutely still, and when we were trying to move silently over the rounded summit of Meall Mor, Donald came out with, 'Anna – would you mind keeping yer legs a bit further apart?'

Even he, speedy and skilful as he was, could not always find stags, and often a day turned out blank. Then our luck would suddenly change, and everything would go right – as on a morning when he, David Lyon and I struck out left-handed from the glen road and walked up Stob Mhic-Bheathain. Soon we spotted a herd of about twenty stags. A quick stalk, and David shot one, a moderate beast with a poor head. Then, as we began to drag it down to the road, we saw the same lot below us, moving east. While I stayed behind, the other two ran forward at a crouch and dropped into a firing position. Donald selected another poor stag, and David shot it – whereupon the rest of the bunch bolted a short way downhill, but then stopped, with fatal results for a third beast. So, within the space of a few minutes, we had three stags – two six-pointers and a switch – all well off the forest.

Second stalkers came and went, none better than young Steven McKenzie, who as a boy had lost the sight in one eye – shot by his brother with an air-gun – but nevertheless spotted deer through his monocular with amazing acuity, and often exclaimed, 'There's an absolute *cracker* of a stag ... Oh – a real thumper!' Another favourite of ours was Chris Ogilvie, a keen huntsman with foot-packs in the Lake District, whose calm, gentlemanly manner concealed tremendous enthusiasm for the hill.

One indispensable member of the staff was Donald's wife Trish, a first-class cook and organiser. She not only laid on sumptuous breakfasts and dinners, but rose magnificently to the occasion whenever we held a ceilidh in the big hall, producing lasagne and sundry puddings for thirty or forty people. After a good deal of eating and drinking – and, once, an excellent conjuring show organised by David – dancing broke out. Once, well primed myself, and feeling chivalrous, I was unwary enough to take the floor with Mary, the assistant cook who was (I guess) in her sixties. Too late, I realised that she had hit the vodka a fearful crack, and it needed all my strength to stop her pitching headlong to the floor. The best moments of the evening came when Chris Ogilvie entranced the company with a song and a few airs on his pipes.

Our operations became even more long-ranging when the Guthries rented stalking from Robin Maclean of Ardgour, the laird of the forest next-door to the south. Robin's nearest beat was Glen Scaddle, lying almost parallel with Conaglen, and running east and west. At its far end it divided into three, and the terrain out there was exceedingly rugged and steep. The summit of its most dramatic hill, Sgurr Dhomhnuill (pronounced Donald) was in view from the windows of our lodge, but it stood out so clearly that one could hardly believe that the conical peak was eight miles away. Its name – meaning Donald's Rocky Peak – derived from the romantic story of Donald Maclean the first of Ardgour, a fifteenth-century hunter of legendary powers who was gored to death by a stag on the eastern slopes of the mountain. So precipitous are its flanks that one of our American visitors got stuck at a very exposed point: not having the strength to keep finding foot- and hand-holds, she lost her nerve, and for several minutes was unable to move at all: she could only cling to the rock like a limpet, until she relaxed enough to let us help her down. On faces of that ferocity it was often impossible to take a shot, because a dead beast would have gone over a precipice and smashed itself to pulp on the rocks below.

Over the next ridge from Glen Scaddle, to the south, lay Glen Gour itself, even wilder and higher, and approached by a truly appalling road, which rivalled the track up the side of Loch Etive in its power to disembowel even the most robust vehicle. Days in Glen Gour were always exciting, but bound to be marathons, because of the length of the outward and inward treks beyond the end of the track.

At Conaglen, when we came in from the hill we generally repaired

to the large, plank-lined gunroom in the back of the lodge for a beer
or a dram, and on miserable wet days somebody would cheer the
place up by lighting the fire. Our sessions, always convivial, were often
cut short by a peremptory call of 'Dinner's up!', but once I inadvisedly
went off with Donald to do some competitive butchery in the stag
larder – a contest which ended with me taking a small slice off the end
of one finger.

Now and then an evening in the gunroom was enlivened by the
presence of a visitor – and none was more entertaining than Alan
Macpherson, a retired Head Stalker, who had worked at Conaglen for
more than thirty years, and told splendid stories of the past. The best
concerned a day when the rifle was Mrs M., the wife of the laird, and
a formidable character. On a wet morning, together with Mrs M. and
Sandy the ghillie, Alan set out on foot up the glen and walked steadily
for an hour, spying the faces on either side. As usual, he was carrying
the rifle, and Mrs M. stayed close at his heel, eager for blood. Then,
spying stags on their left, they struck off up the hill.

Two hours out from home, disaster: suddenly in his mind's eye
Alan saw the box of .270 cartridges standing on the mantelpiece in the
gunroom. He had put it there ready, but now he had a dreadful feeling
he had never picked it up. Surreptitiously he ran his hands over his
jacket pockets: nothing. He had left the ammunition behind.

What to do? For a few moments he kept climbing as he wrestled
with the problem. Then he decided: no – it would too humiliating to
admit his mistake and turn back. So at the next halt he drew Sandy
aside on the pretext of discussing the ground ahead and told him the
bad news.

'Will I go back for it?' Sandy asked.

'Ach, no – ye'd never catch us again.' Then he said: 'Listen. We'll
carry on, no bother. And if we get into a stalk, I'll pretend to put one
up the spout. Just as she's about to fire, ye'll jump up and put the stags
away.'

With that agreed, they went on, and presently they *did* get into
some stags: stalker and rifle left Sandy behind and crept up within

range of four good beasts on a rock-strewn face, Alan went through the motions of loading a round into the breach, sliding the bolt quietly backwards and forwards; but he took good care to keep hold of the rifle as they crawled the last few yards into a firing position.

'The stag on the left, Madam,' he whispered, handing the weapon over. 'He's tail-on to you now, but when he turns, take him.'

Mrs M. settled herself in position. The chosen stag continued to feed calmly away from them, and then, step by step, began turning broadside. But just as she was about to aim, the deer suddenly bolted. Twisting his head round for a peep behind him, Alan saw Sandy capering like a lunatic on the skyline.

'What happened?' exclaimed Mrs M., in some annoyance. 'What put them off?'

'Must have had a puff of our wind, Madam.'

'They can't have! It's coming straight from them.'

'Aye, here it is. But the wind is awful tricky on this face.'

With that he turned his head again, as if checking the direction of the breeze, and was relieved to find that Sandy was nowhere to be seen.

'Never mind,' he said. 'We'll try again.'

And so they did: an hour later, another stalk, into a bigger bunch of stags; another crawl. This time Alan had not quite handed the rifle over when the deer were suddenly threw up their heads and were away like blazes. Alan did not dare look round again, but he knew Sandy had done another Highland fling on the horizon.

'Oh, damn them!' he said loudly.

Mrs M. said something worse, and again demanded peremptorily to know what had gone wrong.

'It's the time of year, Madam, with the rut coming on. The stags is awful jumpy just now.'

Soon after that the rain set in more heavily, and the party decided to turn for home. As they drew near the lodge, wet through after a long and dispiriting trudge, Mrs M. said, 'Give me the rifle, Alan. I'll put it by the Aga to dry.'

'Ach no, Madam, I'll need to give it a good run-through and strip it down.'

'Nonsense! I'll take it' – and she made as it to lay hold of it.

Somehow he parried her attempts, and regained the gunroom still in possession, while Mrs M. went off to have a hot bath. But for days afterwards he remained uneasy, for although he *thought* he had got away with the deception, he feared that when Mrs M. looked back over the sequence of events, she might still become suspicious.

One drawback of Conaglen was the disappointing quality of the fishing. During our first years we did catch a few salmon in the Cona, and one or two in the Scaddle, the river in the neighbouring glen, where we had rights on certain days. But once fish farms were established in Loch Linnhe, close to both estuaries, the number of wild salmon returning to the rivers dwindled almost to nothing. Nevertheless, there were still fish to be caught – if you knew how to catch them. One morning our friend Alison Gibbs found a fine, fresh salmon lying on the bank, with a chunk bitten out of it by an otter. Quickly lighting a fire with driftwood, she broiled it there and then, and other fisherfolk congregated from distant points on the river to enjoy a delicious supplement to their pieces.

A greater problem than shortage of fish was the ever-rising expense of taking the forest. Even with the rent spread among all the families involved, we began to feel the strain, and looked for ways of defraying the cost. Strange as it sounds, we minimised the problem by taking on yet more ground.

Beyond Loch Shiel, to the west, lay a compact forest called Glenaladale, only 12,500 acres, but stunningly attractive and remote, with no road access to its central glen, which could be reached only by boat. I happened to know the owner, Hugh Cheape, a distinguished Gaelic scholar, piper and museum curator, and he kindly allowed us to take some of the stalking without also renting his lodge at Slatach, hard by Glenfinnan at the head of Loch Shiel. This meant that stags were half the price of those at Conaglen, and that we could send out a third stalking party every day – which in turn meant that our team could be larger and that individual contributions could be slightly reduced.

So began a new era, in which a detachment of three or four people would drive off early in the morning to a setting full of history and romance – for it was at Glenfinnan that Bonnie Prince Charlie landed when he came from France in his quest to regain the throne at the start of the 1745 rebellion. Today the event is commemorated by a slender, round tower standing on a fine site by the head of the loch (dismissed by Queen Victoria as 'a very ugly monument to Prince Charles Edward, looking like a sort of lighthouse'). Even more familiar to thousands of film-goers is the Victorian railway viaduct which curves round the hill at the back of the bay, and featured strongly in the Harry Potter sagas.

During the first season of our new arrangement we had breakfast at a pub on the main road, where we were maddened by the incessant piped music (when we asked the waitress to turn it off, she said that silence was impossible, as it might 'upset the residents'). Then, with the advent of a new stalker at Slatach, Davy McAuley, we did far better, with splendid breakfasts of porridge, eggs, bacon and black pudding cooked by his wife, Catrina.

The original lodge – a large Victorian building strongly reminiscent of the house at Conaglen – had become a hotel, and Hugh Cheape had supplanted it with a modern Colt bungalow almost on the shore of the loch. Having fuelled up in this cosy base, we would board the estate's powerful, diesel-engined boat and set off down the loch. On still mornings the voyage was pure delight: sunlight flashed off the surface, great rock-faces slid past on either hand, and range after range of hills folded down to the water, one beyond the other, for twenty miles ahead. Eight miles from base, as we came past a shoulder, Glenaladale itself would gradually open up into view on our right – a magnificent valley striking deep into the hills – and as soon as Davy had moored the boat to a wooden pier, we would go ashore to start walking up a track into the interior. A mile up the glen there was one house which the laird had rescued from oblivion and made just about habitable, for occasional occupation. From there we would spy the heights all round and plan the day's manoeuvres, eating the odd blackberry from a bush that straggled against a stone wall, survivor of some earlier occupation.

Davy – short and stocky, with close-cropped dark hair, always irrepressibly cheerful, and as highly skilled in handling the boat as he was in working the hill – was well versed in the history of the glen. Three hundred people had once lived here, he told us – a complete community, which included its own tailor – and whenever we climbed the precipitous slopes, we looked down on the sad relics of their endeavours: the outlines of buildings and field-walls, the ridges of the lazy beds in which they grew vegetables. With the human inhabitants long gone, the deer now hold sway – and nowhere more spectacularly than at the upper end of the glen, in Corrie Reidh, a high and terrifically steep bowl flanked by precipices and great rushes of fallen scree, in which one arm of the Aladale river rises. There in early September, before the rut, we could sometimes count 200 stags, taking their ease on its grassy lower slopes.

One feature of the forest that fascinated me was the hill called Beinn Mhic Ceididh, which has the steepest grass face it is possible to imagine, tilted at such an angle that walking across it is extremely difficult. In my experience most seriously steep faces consist of rock, but this one is of short grass, and much favoured by the deer, which negotiate it with ease. Not so an aggressively fit young woman who joined our stalking party one morning – I am not sure why – and made herself objectionable by taking violent exercise every time we stopped for a breather. No sooner had we halted, panting, than she would go into a routine of jumps, squats, step-ups, push-ups, burpees and sundry other contortions, clearly implying that we were a bunch of clapped-out crocks. Yet when it came to crossing the face of Beinn Mhic Ceididh, she was defeated: stricken by vertigo, and unable to walk, she was humiliated by having to crawl.

Every stalk in the forest involved a tough initial climb, but one of the most agreeable ascents was the route known as Mrs Young's path, named after an earlier owner who, in about 1905, had a zig-zag track carved out of the side of a corrie on the western side of the glen for the benefit of his wife, a keen but over-weight stalker. Although now only a foot wide in places, the path still takes the ferocity out of the climb by lessening the gradient on each little section, and brings you gently up to a large, relatively level plateau known as the Gaskan Flats, where you can still see the remains of the sheilings which the glen folk built on their summer pastures.

It was as we came down off the flats one evening that I suffered a major setback. We were not using the path, because we had got a stag, and Davy was dragging it straight down a very steep face strewn with boulders and pitted with hollows, all half hidden by rough vegetation. The descent was so uncomfortable that I unhitched my binoculars from round my neck and stowed them in the shoulder bag in which I carried my piece and a spare jersey – only to find when I reached the bottom that the glasses had fallen out somewhere on the way down. The loss was severe: they were a first-class pair, Zeiss 7 x 56s, and had cost some £700 – and although I came down that face several times more on later days, always trying to follow my original line, I never found them.

The difficulties of getting to and from Glenaladale, and of recovering stags from its further reaches – especially if two were got on the same day – emerge vividly from one of Katy's diary entries:

David [Lyon] pulled that stag down while Davy ran for the Argo. I added rifle to current load. David and Danny [the ghillie] instructed to ring and say we'd be late for dinner (and collect some beer). We walked down to the pier in the dusk of a fine evening and then pitch dark. Lots of murky bog to tumble into. Then the stars came out and the moon rose. Magic.

Waited at the pier for them to bring back the big boat – stags still there on the pier in Argo. Fine, warm night, owls hooting, small animals rustling and screeching. Then in chugged the boat, lights blazing, and Duncan [another ghillie] aboard (great to see

him again) wearing a handy-looking miner's lamp on his head.
Loaded stags on front and home we went, Davy doing some
skilled navigation in the dark, as lots of small islands and rocks
were sticking out of the low loch. Reached the lodge by 10 pm
and back at Conaglen by 11 pm.

Any of our party who could not face the Glenaladale hills were always
welcome to fish on Loch Shiel, and many a picnic took place on an
attractive little beach tucked into the western shore. The loch contained salmon as well as trout, and on Saturdays, when fishing
competitions were held, the surface came alive with small boats scudding or drifting in all directions. Among the enthusiasts who took part
was Donnie Strang, one-time second stalker at Conaglen, a skilled
angler who often ran out the winner, with the greatest weight of fish.
One morning he spotted David Lyon and me walking up into the
plantation at Slatach on a private but perfectly legitimate extra stalk to
see if we could get one of the stags that had been damaging the trees.
Standing upright in his boat in mid-loch, Donnie let fly a cry of 'Away,
ye poaching buggers!' – at which I was sorely tempted to put a bullet
into the water close by him, if not through the bows of his vessel.

Davy told a marvellous story of a failed mission to bury a funeral
urn on the hill called Croit Bheinn, far down the loch on the right-
hand side. The ashes in question were the remains of a man who had
loved that mountain, and had asked for them to be placed on the top.
To perform these last rites, two ghillies were despatched down Loch
Sheil in a rowing boat, armed with the urn in a wooden casket and
a bottle of whisky to keep them going.

During the voyage the weather turned foul, with tearing wind
and rain, so they repeatedly fortified themselves from the bottle, to
the point at which the idea of climbing the hill became insufferable
and they decided that nobody would ever know if they sank the casket
in the middle of the loch. They therefore threw it overboard; but
they had not realised that it would float, and to their dismay they saw
the wind taking it away from them, bobbing on the waves. If it

came ashore, and somebody found it ... Rowing frantically, but unable to catch it, they decided that the only remedy was to open fire on it with their .22 rifle – by which unorthodox method they eventually managed to send the ashes to their last resting place.

We were extremely fortunate, in that, as well as Glenaladale, we had yet another outlet for our energy in the form of occasional forays down the Morvern peninsula, to the far west. These were organised by Iain Thornber, an exceptionally knowledgeable professional stalker, and a historian of wide repute, with wonderful knowledge of the hill, the deer and local affairs past and present. Living at Lochaline on the Sound of Mull, he knew all the ground between there and Kingairloch, fifteen miles to the east, and through his agency we negotiated to shoot the occasional stag on the Ardtornish estate.

Every expedition made in his company was memorable. We would set off from Conaglen by car and drive down past Ardgour, the terminal of the Corran ferry (where, in the primitive, roofless urinal, we once found an inspired slogan. Someone had scrawled on the wall 'Ethnic cleansing for Ardnamurchan' – ridiculous in itself, as no coloured person had ever been seen down the peninsula – but corrected by some other hand so that it read 'HARpic cleansing ...').

Leaving behind that twitch of civilisation, we went on through wild mountains to Kingairloch, where Robin Maclean moored the motor-cruiser *Cathula*, which he owned jointly with Iain, by the jetty at the head of a long inlet called Loch Corrie. Comfortably embarked, we proceeded down the coast to land on the estuary at the mouth of the Glensanda river or, further on, at Eignaig, the bay of the oaks, an enchanted spot where (Iain conjectured) ships may have been built and launched from the steep shingle beach during the Middle Ages. There among the trees stood a little cottage, and because its facilities were limited, someone had set up a fully flushing, gleaming white lavatory on a plinth some distance from the house. Anyone using it sat enthroned among the oaks, several feet above the ground.

While we stalked, Robin stood off in the boat, gradually moving down the coast as he spied deer movements and reported them to us by radio. If we got a stag, we had to drag it down to the shore, and Robin, having anchored the *Cathula* a short distance out, would row a red inflatable dinghy in to pick us up. One of the best hours of my life came when, after a long, hard day and a blistering struggle to pull a stag down a cliff choked with brambles, bracken and hawthorn, we floated serenely on a silver sea, drinking ice-cold gins-and-tonics, eating small pork pies, and watching inquisitive seals pop up all round with eyes bulging and whiskers bristling, while across the bay the ruin of Ardtornish castle stood out in silhouette, black against a flaring sunset.

Iain made an ideal companion on the hill, always ready with a snippet of legend or a stalking anecdote, and particularly good on the strange, almost mystical experiences one has when out in the Highlands – for instance that of approaching a skyline and knowing in detail what you are going to see beyond it, even though you have never been there before. He sent shivers up my spine by describing how he once heard what in old Gaelic lore was known as *Oiteag sluaigh* – the breeze of the host of the dead:

> At one moment it sounded like heavy breathing, and at another like a child crying in pain. It is a sound sometimes heard by shepherds and stalkers in the high corries, as eerie as it is unexpected. It was known to the Romans, who wrote of its meaning in these islands.

No one could stalk in Morvern during the 1980s without getting wind of that tantalising mystery of modern times – the disappearance of Arthur Strutt. Laird of the 23,000-acre Kingairloch Estate, Strutt was last seen alive one morning in 1977, when, at the age of sixty-nine, he walked out of the house with a couple of pruning saws to do some brashing – the removal of side branches from young trees – in a sitka spruce plantation close to the lodge. Because he was a man of regular habits, his failure to return for lunch caused immediate alarm. His family searched the house and gardens, and then called in the police, who arrived after dark. They too scoured the policies that night, and for several nights thereafter members of the family took turns to sit out in the woods, listening for distress calls, thinking that Strutt might have broken a leg and be shouting for help.

Phenomenal efforts were made to find the missing man. More than a dozen wider searches were launched by the estate staff, by the army, and by experienced members of the Lochaber Mountain Rescue team from Fort William, who combed the area with their trained dogs. All drew blank. In some places the plantation was so thick that the searchers had to crawl, and several of them had their new Goretex jackets ripped to shreds. Andy Nichol, leader of the Lochaber team, took along his own Alsatian, which he had taught to bark when it found a casualty, alive or dead, and he knew the dog would give tongue if it discovered anything. Even when the urgency of the initial searches had died down, he returned several times at weekends to have a further hunt on his own.

Inevitably, rumours began to circulate: that for some reason Strutt had done a bolt and gone abroad; that he had been kidnapped or murdered; that he had fallen into the river and drowned; that he had been lusting after a maid in Kingairloch House, and because she had repulsed his advances, he had committed suicide. A clairvoyant in England reported that he was definitely alive. The police took a keen interest, because several other highland lairds had recently been murdered by members of their staff. The only certain fact was that he had vanished. Three years later local speculation increased when details of his will were published, showing that he had left £1,233,000, and the family took legal proceedings to have him declared officially dead so that the money could be released.

Then, in 1982, came the astounding *dénouement*. Five years after his disappearance, the family held a memorial service in the church at Kingairloch, and *the very next day* his remains were discovered in a plantation by a forestry worker prospecting the route for a new road. Only five hundred yards from the house, his skeleton, still clad in his old clothes, was propped in a sitting position against the base of a tree, half buried by fallen spruce needles; his cheap Timex watch was still on the bones of his left wrist, and the two hand-saws lay beside him, together with a ball-point pen. The only sign of anything wrong was that he had taken off his neckerchief and hung it on a branch of the spruce against which he was lying – which suggested that he might have felt short of breath and suffered a heart attack. But because in five years the tree had grown a good deal, the cravat was two or three feet above him – and it was this that had attracted the forestry worker's attention.

To Dr Bill Masson, who was summoned to examine the remains, it seemed – and still seems – astonishing that all the earlier searches had failed to find him. Also very strange, in the doctor's view, was the fact that his skeleton had remained intact: almost always the remains of a casualty are scattered by scavenging badgers and foxes. 'Not a single bone was missing,' the doctor recalled. 'Even the little bones of the fingers were all present.' The skeleton had been picked clean by insects, except at the bottom of the legs, inside wellington boots, where the flesh was still not fully decomposed.

Having collected the bones in a sack, the doctor took them to Kingairloch House, with a policeman and the Procurator Fiscal in attendance. When he showed the watch to Arthur's widow, Patricia, she immediately identified it as having belonged to her husband – and when she wound it up, it started at once. Then she said, 'Gentlemen, this calls for a drink' – and out came a silver tray bearing tumblers and a bottle of whisky.

Patricia Strutt was one of the most formidable lady deer-stalkers of all time. Modelling herself on that other demon Highland huntress, Alma, Marchioness of Breadalbane – whose book of reminiscences *The High Tops of Black Mount* was first published in 1898 and remains a classic of stalking literature to this day – Mrs Strutt trained for the hill like an Olympic athlete. To prepare for every season she went on daily, four-mile hill walks, and crawled about her bedroom floor to strengthen her stomach muscles.

Another peculiarity was her habit of collecting cartridge cases. If she had to fire two shots to kill a stag, she did not bother to pick up the empties; but if a single shot sufficed (as it usually did) she would spend any amount of time rummaging in the heather for the case, which would finish up as part of a kind of armoured dado that ran round the walls of her bedroom. For her eightieth birthday treat she travelled down to Pipewell Hall, in Northamptonshire, to take delivery of a new David Lloyd .25.06 rifle, maintaining that she was the only woman in Europe who had sold her Granny Bonds to buy a weapon. She was a little disappointed when firing out of the hut on the maker's test-range that she could not quite get all her shots through the same hole on the target; but on the hill she was deadly, and she went on stalking until failing eyesight finally ended her career at the age of eighty-eight, by which time she had killed more than 2000 stags. One day, out with Iain Thornber, she killed two stags within eight seconds, each with a bullet in the neck, at a range of 180 yards.

Around Kingairloch it was common knowledge that she and her husband had not been on the best of terms before he disappeared. People said that in the evenings they sat on either side of the fire in the living room, each armed with a private supply of whisky, arguing about the ownership of individual bottles, and each marking the levels with pencils to stop the other cheating. When Arthur's skeleton was found, scandalous rumours got about, to the effect that she had somehow had him poisoned – even that she had secreted his body in a deep-freeze until the searches died down, and then had had it put out on the spot where it was eventually found. This was pure fantasy – but as the skeleton was cremated, no forensic deductions could be made. Even if she did know something more about Arthur's demise, the secret went with her when she herself died in June 2000 at the age of 89, leaving nearly £3 million in her will.

Unexplained disappearances are not uncommon in the Highlands – and very uncomfortable if they occur in a place that you know well. Another took place one winter in Glenaladale, when a small team

went out to stay in the house in the glen for a couple of nights, the aim
being to cull as many hinds as possible. After supper on the first night
one of the three went out for a walk up the river – and was never seen
again. As at Kingairloch, huge searches took place. The stalkers from
neighbouring forests walked in over the marches; police and mountain rescue teams searched the glen; helicopters with heat-seeking
equipment flew patrols, and frogmen checked the hollow banks of
the river and the loch. The man was never accounted for, and in the
end most people assumed that, for whatever reason, he had done a
runner, walking out through the top end of the glen, over a pass and
down to the main road. But, as the estate-owner Hugh Cheape
remarked, the incident left everyone concerned with a sense of pro-
found disquiet.

15

Letterewe

OF ALL THE FORESTS IN which I have been lucky enough to stalk, the wildest and most desolate is Letterewe, in Wester Ross – 100,000 acres of rock, peat-bog and water, with scant vegetation and very few trees. I went there several times not as the leader of a family party, but as the guest and friend of a remarkable man, Paul Fentener van Vlissingen.

Tall, blond and blue-eyed, Paul could easily have passed for an Englishman. In fact he was Dutch, but his mother was English, and it was she who gave him his first sight of the Highlands when she took him to Scotland on holiday at the age of eight or nine. Having seen those mountains, he never forgot them, and as he grew up he became increasingly disappointed and angered by what he called the 'gradual urbanisation' of the Dutch countryside. In his youth his family had owned one of the largest tracts of wild land in Holland, the 10,000-acre forest known as the *Planken Wambuis* (literally Wooden Shirt); but when they sold the land in the 1950s, it was, in his own words, 'opened up like Disneyland, with paved roads and signs on every corner, so that it became practically a theme park.' As he remarked, political correctness reached such a stage that if 'you're detected so much as setting a mouse-trap, the Greens come and camp in your drive.'

Luckily he had the means to seek wild places elsewhere. As the ninth-generation chief executive of SHV, a family wholesale business, he controlled an enterprise employing more than 50,000 people in Europe, the Far East and other parts of the globe, and at least twice a year he went round the world by private jet, calling on senior managers. His wealth was immense, and that, combined with his energy, his keen intellect and passion for wilderness, set him looking for an estate to buy. In February 1977, when he heard from a friend that Letterewe was for sale, he flew to Inverness and drove rapidly westwards to look at it. Because he had not realised that there is no road access to most of the forest, and in any case snow was lying, all he could do was to skirt round the edges, buying drams for locals in pubs and asking discreet questions about the possibility of a sale.

Without having set foot on the ground, he bought the estate from the previous owners, the Whitbread brewing family, of whom Colonel Bill Whitbread had long been the figurehead. The Colonel was well known in the fields of racing (he had twice ridden in the Grand National) and of ocean-going yachts, having founded the Round-the-World race in 1973. He had a reputation for being both cantankerous and eccentric, and it was said that whenever he moved from one house to another – a frequent occurrence – he would take his kitchen table with him. He was also a lifelong deer-stalker: he bought Letterewe from the Zetland family in 1947 and cherished the estate for thirty years, more or less setting aside Fisherfield, the far, northern part of the forest, as his private reserve, to which he would retire for a week or two every autumn with his latest girlfriend.

Paul already had a fine estate in the south – Conholt Park, in Hampshire, where he created one of the best pheasant shoots in England – and now his new possession more than fulfilled his longing for wilderness. The main lodge, Letterewe itself, which stands on the northern shore of Loch Maree, is accessible only by boat, and two lesser lodges, far in the hinterland, are even more gloriously remote. Carnmore, an eight mile walk away from Letterewe, is at the head of the lovely Fionn Loch – the White Loch – approached by a causeway between its eastern end and the smaller Dubh-Lochain. Larachanti-vore, seventeen miles out, looks down over Loch na Sealga – the Hunters' Loch – with the towering bulk of An Teallach commanding the northern horizon. The sky-lines around both houses are awe-inspiring. There is no road to either: humans reach the lodges on foot, but stores have to go in by boat.

Urged on by his partner, the writer Caroline Tisdall-Mackenzie, Paul soon turned himself into a model laird. At first traditionalists resented the arrival of a foreign millionaire, but they quickly came into line when they saw that his over-riding aim was to preserve the wilderness in its pristine state. Not only did he walk every acre of the forest: he learnt the Gaelic names of every hill and corrie, every burn and lochan, and he knew what every name meant. He also resisted attempts to open up the estate with new roads and camp-sites, and after some bitter arguments he won widespread agreement with the Letterewe Accord, which established good relations between all parties, granting access to walkers, campers and climbers provided they respected the environment and stayed off the ground on week-days during the all-important deer cull in autumn.

Paul's most burning interest was in the deer. A tireless walker, and a first-class shot, he employed four professional stalkers, and himself went out with them all over the forest, culling poor-quality beasts of both sexes in a determined effort to improve the quality of the herd. After a few years the results of his dedication could be seen in the astonishing museum which he established: the antlers and jaw-bones of every stag shot on the estate, carefully cleaned and numbered, were displayed in a former cow-byre, hung over the rafters, nailed up and down the walls and spread out in rows on the floor. The massed ranks made a macabre sight, but they told a revealing story. From the spindly, stick-like heads of early seasons, the antlers steadily improved, gaining points and thickness in the beam, to a level at which the stalkers began to have a job finding stags poor enough to shoot. Every head had been photographed by Barbara, wife of the Head Stalker, Graeme Grant, and the weight and age of the beast recorded.

Paul's policy was never to cull the big, mature stags which would be typical targets on more conventional estates, but to take out any animal with a poor head or body, no matter how young or old it was. He also advocated the Continental practice of shooting hinds and calves at the same time, and called for the start of the hind season to be brought forward from 1st November to 1st September, so that young calves could be despatched more easily. If this policy sounded brutal, it was founded in common sense – for, as he pointed out, a calf which lost its mother in November suffered both physically and mentally, in that it was deprived of its most nutritious food – her milk – for at least two months of the winter, and (no less important) as an orphan it came under intolerable social pressure in the herd, which meant that it would probably do poorly all its life.

Paul often likened his culling to that of wolves, which had been exterminated from Scotland during the eighteenth century. Wolves, he pointed out, usually pulled down the oldest and weakest members of a herd, thus ensuring the survival of the fittest, and he frequently advocated the re-introduction of wolves as a means of reducing the ever-rising deer population, in spite of the problems major carnivores would cause among sheep-farmers and hikers. To back up his own theories and researches, he commissioned a three-year scientific study and published a hefty report.

He himself often went to the hill accompanied by two deer-hounds, Tuesday and Wednesday, which he and Caroline had acquired. Harking back a hundred years to the time when the use of such dogs had been common, he trained them to crawl behind him or Caroline in the final stages of a stalk, and after a shot he would loose them off, to race on to the stricken beast. He was profoundly interested in the scenting powers of dogs in general, and at one stage acquired a Bavarian Mountain Stalking dog – a kind of jumbo Dachs-hund, called Piglet – which had a phenomenally keen nose.

As an experiment he got one of the stalkers to lay a trail by drag-ging a sack of deer offal in a long loop round some low ground beside Loch Maree. His first idea was to leave it all day, and try the dog on it in the evening; but then he changed his mind, and said they would hold the trial next morning. During the night torrential rain came on, and the stalkers felt sure that every trace of the drag must have been washed away – but no: the dog picked up the line at once, and fol-lowed it to the end. Caroline was delighted when her deerhound out-ployed even this specialist tracker. Out stalking on the hill, Wednesday deviated from the line of advance and went up a short dis-tance on her own, to show her human companions a single cigarette butt, deposited there ten days earlier by an Austrian who had just gral-loched a stag.

An invitation to stalk at Letterewe was a ticket to another world, in which the harshness of the environment was counter-balanced by the sybaritic comforts of the main lodge. The house, which Paul and Caroline had completely refurbished, had every amenity; and if the food, prepared by the Dutch chef, was rich and delicious beyond description, the wine was positively celestial. Paul himself usually drank only Château Ducru Beaucaillou, but all the claret was superla-tive, whether Château Palmer or Château Cheval Blanc.

On my first visit Paul greeted me with the startling news, 'We're sending you out to Carnmore,' he said. 'You'll be there on your own, but I'm sure you'll manage.' So, after one luxurious night at Letterewe, we were away, driving along Loch Maree, out to the sea and up the coast, before turning back inland along the rough track that leads to the western end of the Fionn Loch. There Dougie Russell, the Carn-more stalker, was awaiting me – a small, wiry man, who ferried me up the loch to the lodge. The little grey house, hunched against the foot of a steep, rock-bound crag, looked welcoming, but I hardly had time to deposit my kit inside it before we were off on our first stalk.

This proved short and relatively painless. I was delighted when we set out along the shore of the loch, for I knew something about the hill ahead of us, Beinn a' Chaisgein Beag, the Little Hill of Cheese, from my earlier reading, and had long wanted to see it. It was here that the great naturalist Frank Fraser Darling came to study the deer in the 1930s; here that he went barefoot for a summer to feel the pulse of the country more clearly, and here, as he lay on the western slopes of the hill, that he heard 'the singing of women's voices and the laughter of little children.' Maybe, he thought, it was 'the play of wind and falling water' which made these sounds, but he did not care: he 'was content to listen to the beauty of the moment.'

Fate decreed that although I saw the hill, I never climbed it, for earlier in the day Dougie had spied an old stag on its own not far from the loch-side, and we found it again easily enough. A careful stalk, an easy shot, and that was that. Just as well, for although the day had been fine, the weather was working itself up into a major storm, and as we regained the lodge, a full gale was howling in from the west. Dougie's last words before he disappeared into the gathering darkness were, 'The old house'll talk to you tonight' – and with that he was gone, leaving me alone.

Five garron ponies, three white, two dun, were grazing on the open ground in front of the lodge, and I wondered why they didn't take shelter in the barn down by the shore. Then, as a burst of rain came flying up the loch, they did move off, and I went inside.

How strange and difficult to have no electricity! The dark pine panelling on walls and ceiling, the bare wood floor, the kitchen dresser – everything seemed to soak up the last glimmers of daylight. The solid-fuel Rayburn was burning well, and the water was hot, but the shadows were so deep that I had trouble finding a match to light one of the oil lamps. When I got one going, its harsh yellow light revealed a kettle on the calor gas stove and a tin of tea-bags on a shelf; so I got a brew on while I explored the house. In the little sitting-room a fire had been laid in the grate, with kindling and coal. In the store-room there was a sack of potatoes on the concrete floor, and the gas-powered fridge in the kitchen contained eggs, milk and a pack of bacon. At least I wasn't going to starve – and, early though it was, I thought I should maybe start preparing supper.

As I drank a mug of tea, for some reason I began to feel nervous. Already Dougie's prediction was coming true. The old house had begun to talk. Bursts of rain were rattling on the windows. The wind was thundering on the roof and booming in the chimneys. The panelling creaked, a door swung open with the draught. When the kettle on the gas ring gave a sudden squeal, I jumped, thinking I had heard a human voice.

I seemed to be hearing other noises, too – an engine (impossible, as there was no road within miles), the howl of a dog (no less unlikely). What I *could* hear was the intermittent roaring of stags, which had come down close behind the house, and sounded as if they were challenging the storm rather than each other. Suddenly that howl (or whatever it had been) set me thinking of the great grey dog of Meoble – a legendary creature with an unearthly, wailing cry.

I knew the outlines of its story: how early in the nineteenth century the animal's owner Dugald Macdonald had gone away to the wars, and in his absence the bitch had given birth to four pups on an island in a hill loch. Returning, Dugald had made straight for the island, but the mother was away hunting, and the half-grown pups, not knowing him, tore him to pieces. When his remains were interred in the cemetery at the mouth of the Meoble River, the bitch came and howled over his grave, until one day she was found lying dead beside it – after which her spectral appearances were said to presage the death of members of the Macdonald clan in South Morar.

Even as my scalp began to prickle, I knew why the story had come into my mind. It was just that I had seen Paul's deerhounds, which were brindled and shaggy, that morning. All the same, something made me re-load my rifle, which was standing in the corner by the door.

Into my mind came another remark of Fraser Darling's, about how there were places in the Highlands from which he had felt impelled to move out at nightfall – not from fear, but from some unidentifiable 'discomfort' strong enough to shift him. As the gale roared and the old house shuddered, I began to feel claustrophobia closing in on me. Panic was threatening. Dog or no dog, gale or no gale, I had to get outside. With the rifle in one hand, I opened the door – only to be hit by such a blast of rain and wind that I was practically blown back in again. In a few seconds I was dripping with water, so I rapidly withdrew and slammed the door on the storm.

That sudden, ice-cold shower brought me to my senses, and all at once I analysed what my trouble was: it was simply that I was severed from all contact with the outside world. I had no means of communication with any other human being. Without even a transistor radio, I could not summon up a human voice out of the darkness. I realised that a hundred years ago, before the advent of electricity, telephones and radio, all country people had lived in this state. Once night came down, they were cut off in their homes, and did not expect to hear or speak to anyone else until daylight returned.

This truth – so obvious when articulated – banished my alarm. I unloaded the rifle and returned it to its corner, lit more lamps and got on with the business of preparing supper. And then, as I peeled some potatoes, I remembered the wine. 'In the cupboard under the stairs,' Paul had told me, 'you'll find some fairly decent claret. I hope it's all right.'

All right! By God – here was an astonishing cornucopia: Château la Lagune, Château Palmer, Château Pichon-Lalande. As my torch-beam picked out the labels, I could scarcely believe my eyes. Handling it reverently, I chose a bottle of Château Brane-Cantenac, opened it, and set it on the shelf above the stove.

Soon I had potatoes coming to the boil, diced bacon sizzling in a frying pan and tinned tomatoes warming on another hob. Then, having drained the potatoes and turned the gas-rings down, I went upstairs and had a steaming hot bath before putting on a tracksuit. Thus accoutred, I sat down to a candle-lit supper, accompanied by the Wagnerian clamour of the storm – and even if the food might not have pleased diners at the Ritz, the wine would have sent them into ecstasies. With the whole bottle inside me, I slept like a lamb, all worries forgotten.

In the morning the storm was still raging. The rain was now intermittent, but so much had fallen that all the burns had become boiling white torrents, and the wind was so strong that a waterfall across the loch had turned into a geyser: instead of dropping as it flowed over a lip of rock, the torrent was being blown skywards in huge vertical jets of spray.

Dougie came for me at nine, and instead of opting to lurk in the lodge, which we might honourably have done until the weather cleared, we set out regardless. The rain made spying almost impossible: visibility was wretched, and binoculars were flooded within seconds. At one point, as we both crouched under an overhanging rock to escape a particularly vicious downpour, I said to my companion, 'To think that I'm doing this for fun!'

'Aye,' he replied, 'I'm thinking we're both a bit round the twist!'

Dougie was painfully thin, and I was worried when I found he had brought nothing in the way of a piece. He said he never ate anything in the middle of the day: a sup of water sufficed to keep him going. Yet his stamina was amazing, and he seemed as impervious to the weather as any deer. Our movements that day were much hampered by burns that had become impassable, but late in the afternoon we did manage to close in on a stag – which I missed. The lever of the old Mauser safety-catch, slippery in the wet, did its trick of not going quite down when I wanted to fire, so that it gave out its tiny click, and when I did move it again, the rifle went off prematurely.

That evening Caroline, accompanied by Tuesday and Wednesday, appeared out of the dusk, half-way through a seventeen-mile hike to Larachantivore, where she was to join Paul. Her arrival absolved me from the task of cooking supper: finding two pieces of fillet steak in the fridge, she fried them perfectly, and garnished them with wonderfully crisp potatoes, roasted with rosemary. Our meal was made memorable not only by another astonishing bottle of claret, but also by the presence of the two great hounds, which sat upright on either side of their mistress as we ate, their rough, curly heads on the level of the table-top, and their eyes glinting in the candlelight – a scene straight out of a Landseer painting.

The rest of the week sped past. Each day Dougie and I worked our way out to a different part of the forest, and we saw any number of deer, as well as some grey-and-white wild goats, whose devastating smell nearly knocked us over from far down-wind. There was often a golden eagle in the sky above us, and we once caught the flash of a peregrine, speeding arrow-like along a rock face. But I got only three stags out of a possible five before suddenly it was Friday afternoon, and time to head for base. I could have returned to Letterewe by boat and Land Rover, but out of sheer exuberance I chose to walk over the hill-path carrying my rifle. Five miles further on, in the dark, I was bitterly regretting my decision, and by the time I reached the lodge I looked so exhausted that Paul pressed on me a huge glass of whisky, insisting that I drink it immediately.

That week at Letterewe was one of the best of my life – five days in the majestic wilderness, alone with Dougie, a man whose knowledge of the deer and their environment was immeasurably greater than mine.

No wonder Paul loved Letterewe. During his tenure of almost thirty years he spent millions of pounds on maintaining the forest, and he also contributed with splendid generosity to other Scottish causes, among them the encouragement of the Gaelic language, giving £250,000 to found the Letterewe Scholarships at Sabhal Mòr Ostaig, the National Centre for Gaelic Language and Culture on the Isle of Skye. Many times he repeated his belief that he was never the owner of his land, but only the custodian of it for his lifetime; and his death in 2006 at the age of sixty-five prematurely robbed the Highlands of one its most inspired guardians.

16

Today

A cynic might suggest that although for nearly fifty years I have spent much of my leisure time culling deer, I have not had much success – for now, in 2011, deer numbers in England are the highest in recorded history. I might argue that, besides stalking and doing forestry work, I have written a good deal about deer in various newspapers and journals, promoting their cause and advocating better management. Nevertheless, it is true that, to the alarm of farmers, foresters and conservationists, the total is continuing to grow.

This is certainly a paradox, for in half a century the human population of Britain has expanded from 50 million to 60 million, so that the country is now twice as densely populated as France, and nine times as densely as America. During the same period hundreds of thousands of acres of habitat have been buried under tarmac and concrete – yet the deer have responded by increasing with astonishing vigour. Accurate numbers are hard to establish, but the present population in England alone is thought to be over 800,000, consisting of nearly 500,000 roe, 150,000 fallow, 150,000 muntjac, 50,000 red and 15,000 sika. Even the little Chinese water deer have proliferated to the tune of 10,000. Fallow are reckoned to be increasing at the rate of eight per cent per annum, and muntjac at the alarming pace of twelve per cent.

One place in which deer *have* gained new territory is the National Forest – a tremendous project, which covers two hundred square miles of the Midlands in Derbyshire, Leicestershire and Staffordshire. Some woodland already existed within its boundaries before its inception, but new planting began in the winter of 1990, and by the end of 2008, with more than seven million trees in place, nearly 15,000 acres of farmland, derelict coalfields and mineral workings had been converted into forest. Needless to say, deer quickly began taking advantage of this attractive new range: there were already some fallow in the area before planting began, and now the herd has increased to 300 animals or more.

On a nation-wide scale, the problem is becoming acute, not only because deer do extensive damage to trees, farm crops and gardens: they are also an ever-increasing menace on the roads. At least 50,000 are killed in traffic accidents every year, and many more are so badly injured that although they disappear from the scene, they expire later. About fifteen humans die as a result of these collisions, some 400 are injured, and the cost in damage to vehicles runs into millions of pounds.

Another paradox is that in the past few years the number of trained stalkers has also increased enormously. Training courses run by the British Deer Society and the British Association for Shooting and Conservation are always fully subscribed, and BASC alone has turned out 15,000 trained riflemen. Deer-stalking is now the most rapidly growing field-sport in England, and competition for stalking leases is intense. Yet all these stalkers are failing to keep the deer under control. Another curious fact is that in the south stalking generates very little controversy. Badger-lovers campaign stridently to prevent any cull – to

the chagrin of farmers who have lost their dairy herds to bovine tuber-
culosis. Fox-fanciers continue their bitter opposition to hunting with
hounds. But there is practically no outcry against deer-stalking,
perhaps because people realise that it is a necessity: if no culling were
carried out, the herds would increase by 30 per cent a year, and
damage would beccome intolerable.

The need for good management has never been greater. Hence the
existence of the Deer Initiative, a registered charity with a staff of
fewer than twenty, set up by the Government in 1995, which aims, in
its own words, to maintain 'a sustainable and balanced population of
wild deer' by coordinating the activities of organisations with similar
objectives. It recognises that wild deer 'are an important part of
England's natural resources and play a major role in the economy,
environment and history of England.' It also acknowledges that
'many individuals provide a significant contribution in many forms
towards managing deer populations'. Its *New Deer Leaflet* stresses that
management is necessary to maintain a balance between numbers of
deer and their habitat.

North of the border, the situation is far more volatile, because a
running battle is being fought between those who want to maintain
traditional methods of deer management, and those whose primary
aim is to restore the Caledonian forest. Among the champions of tradition are many Highland estate-owners and the Scottish Gamekeepers' Association (SGA) who point out that red deer are one of
Scotland's most potent tourist attractions, and that the revenue from
sporting lets is essential for the physical care of the environment –
the regular burning of heather, control of predators, maintenance
of estate roads, foot-paths, bridges, and so on. Those who demand
priority for trees include Scottish Natural Heritage (SNH), the Government body charged with care of the environment, and the
National Trust for Scotland.

In overall charge of deer is the Deer Commission, Scotland (DCS),
also a Government organisation. To the rage and dismay of traditionalists, the Commission has often appeared (in the words of one

experienced hill-man) 'to regard deer as Public Enemy No. 1'. In recent years it has become hell-bent on reducing the red deer population as fast as possible, and has condoned or perpetrated fearful massacres, most notably at Glenfeshie early in 2004, and on the National Trust for Scotland estate Mar Lodge in 2005.

At Glenfeshie the Commission brought in a helicopter which drove a herd of some eighty animals up, down and round a hill, creating panic and pushing them into a circle of riflemen. The SGA, having got wind of the plan, managed to infiltrate a cameraman and make a covert video record of the carnage, and its members were outraged not only by the shooting of pregnant hinds out of season, but also by the fact that some of the wounded animals were not finished off for an hour and a half. A further cause of anger was the way in which the carcases were handled, against all the precepts of the code of Best Practice. Such was the scale and haste of the operation that instead of being gralloched on the spot, the bodies were air-lifted intact by helicopter, dumped on farm land covered in sheep droppings, and gralloched there, before being dragged headless across the dirty ground for sale to a game dealer in Perthshire. The whole disgracefully unprofessional proceeding was defended by the authorities on the grounds that the deer had been threatening to destroy a plantation of Scots pine, but its effect was to undermine the Commission's reputation, which was anyway far from enviable.

As I write, in the summer of 2010, the Commission is a separate Government body, but it is about to be merged with SNH – a move likely to pile bureaucracy on bureaucracy. In November 2008 the Commission launched its 'New Approach', aimed at finding ways 'to make the most of the wild deer asset'. But it is hard to have much faith in an organisation which can issue an explanatory statement full of sentences like 'Delivering the strategy actions will contribute to the delivery of other related strategies and policies and the delivery of other strategies will contribute to the wild deer strategy.'

For many years the red deer population did keep increasing, due not least to a series of mild winters and a consequent fall in the number of beasts dying from natural causes in harsh weather. The peak total was thought to be some 350,000. Then, in the winter of 2009–10, Nature struck back with the most vicious spell of weather for twenty years.

In Sutherland the first heavy snowfall came on 14 December. The temperature plummeted to minus 20°C at night, and for three weeks it did not rise about minus 10°C during the day. Three feet of snow blanketed the grass and heather. The hinds' lactation dried up, and so many of their calves starved to death that a whole generation was wiped out. In a paper given at Kingussie on 20 April 2010 to the Annual General Meeting of the Association of Deer Management Groups, Sir Michael Wigan, proprietor of the Borrobol Estate, painted a telling picture of the disaster:

> By New Year stalkers all around were saving deer, not shooting them. Hind stalking was cancelled. [The hinds] ate the hard-type tussock grass right down to the stump, chewed down blaeberry patches on slopes; and they also chewed deer fence posts put in thirty years ago.
>
> When ... the conservation charities exulted in the deer's predicament, claiming it proved their dodgy dogma of over-population, they were sharply rebuffed in the letters columns by local folk who were not deceived, and saw the truth for themselves. This was an old-fashioned lack of available food, then starvation. Had there been a tenth the deer numbers, they would have suffered as much. The food lay intact beneath the frosted snow.
>
> People recoiled at the next instalment: a DCS injunction to continue shooting. Driving tottering hinds back onto crystalline ridges was just too much. The DCS hastily back-tracked, sensing a PR crevasse...
>
> The Sutherland deer massed in railway cuttings because here, on the steep banks, there was vertical, over-hanging vegetation. In one episode on the Inverness–Wick line the train ploughed

into a gathering of deer, killing seventy-seven of them. Linesmen further up found 100 carcases in one place, scattered by 300-ton trains like so many burst cushions.

Sir Michael's address gave out a clear message: that management of the red deer is best left in the hands of men with professional experience. But in the end the climate is the final arbiter.

So much attention has been given to controversy about red deer that in the meantime, almost unnoticed, numbers of roe have quietly crept up to a record level. No one is certain how many there are in Scotland, but some experts believe the total may exceed that of reds, and perhaps be as high as 400,000. Roe are flourishing particularly in the semi-urban areas on the edges of towns, where culling with rifles is dangerous, and they are even being seen in the centre of cities like Glasgow. Sika seem to be stable, at about 20,000, and fallow, in a minority at about 3,000, are not a serious problem. As for barking deer – one terse response to a Commission questionnaire sums up the situation: 'Muntjac must be kept out of Scotland at all cost.'

One big change in most forests has been the advent of all-terrain vehicles, generally known as ATVs. Some lairds prefer to retain the tradional method of bringing deer off the hill with ponies, on the grounds that machines, however light, damage the vegetation and leave tell-tale tracks across grass and heather; but ATVs have generally taken over, and among them one make – the Argocat – has established unchallenged supremacy.

The first Argos, imported in kit form from Canada during the 1970s, were little more than motorised polythene tubs mounted on eight small wheels, all driven by chains. There was room for the driver and one passenger on the front bench seat, and space for four more people or a couple of dead stags in the open back. The controls were primitive, consisting mainly of a couple of hand-levers, right and left, which operated the brakes and the steering – one good yank could turn the vehicle through 180 degrees in its own length. In early versions there was a two-inch gap along either side of the well in the back, and I once saw a sheep-dog leap clean overboard with a tremendous yelp, having lost the tip of its tail, severed by the driving chains.

Later Argos have become more sophisticated and slightly more comfortable, with a larger engine and a bit more space in front; yet from the start they have been incredibly versatile, able to climb forbiddingly steep slopes, scramble over banks and gullies and traverse bogs that would sink conventional vehicles in seconds. One of their secrets is the softness of their tyres and the very low pressure they put on the ground – about 2 lbs per square inch.

They are also amphibious, as I discovered when I gave one a road-test, and was encouraged by the firm distibuting the vehicle to drive it down a hill, flat-out at almost 20 mph, straight into a lake. We hit the water with a wonderful hydraulic deceleration – exactly the feeling (I thought) that a hippo must get when he launches himself into the Limpopo. Our speed through the water was not impressive – only about 1 mph, propulsion being provided by the treads on the tyres – but we reached the far bank safely enough. On the hill Argos have proved invaluable, enabling stalking parties to reach distant beats far more quickly than by any other means, and to recover stags from places which ponies could never reach.

During the years when I was writing a country column which came out on Saturdays in the *Independent*, I always looked keeenly at the calendar for a Saturday that fell on 1st April. One year I had quite some success with my account of the annual rat-shoot in the cellars of Harrods (the season's premier sporting invitation, I claimed), and at the next opportunity I followed up with an account of the Great Argo Race – a marathon event in which the contestants set off from Mallaig, on the west coast of Scotland, along the rocky spine of North Morar, and from there had to motor via various check-points right across the Highlands, finishing at the mouth of the Findhorn. I managed to take in many readers, among them Ian Bond, owner of the North Morar estate, who, when he read the article at his home in

Gloucestershire on Saturday morning, was said to have leapt out of his bath to telephone his factor and the local police, crying 'Get 'em off! Get 'em off!!' – while of course there was nobody on his ground at all. I was glad to hear that he took the spoof in good part.

My fascination with deer has put me in contact with many remarkable hill-men, but none more memorable than that titan among naturalists and wildlife managers, Ronnie Rose. Born in the West Lodge near the castle at Balmoral, where his father was deer-stalker to the royal family, he gained his first glimpses of nature from the game-bag in which his father carried him round the low-ground of the estate on his bicycle. He was brought up among stalkers, gamekeepers and foresters, shot his first red deer hind at the age of ten, left school at fifteen and went to work for the Forestry Commission in the uplands of Central Scotland. From his everyday contact with wild creatures he gained an extraordinary understanding of their lives, and of the interaction between different species, and he saw how essential it is that positive management should balance species in our man-made environment.

Red deer and roe, capercaillie and blackcock – he managed them all with conspicuous success; but no bird better demonstrated the fineness of his understanding than the controversial hen harrier. When he took visitors to see harriers nesting, he would choose a pair of birds which he knew were robust enough to withstand his intrusion, and then provoke them to attack him – which they did, by coming at him like fighter planes with their talons down and snatching off his deer-stalker hat as they passed. One small misjudgement, and his scalp would have been laid open.

His outstanding achievement was the establishment during the 1970s of the huge commercial forest at Eskdalemuir, in Dumfriesshire, which eventually clothed 50,000 acres of poor, hilly farmland with trees. The received wisdom at the time was that conifer plantations could not support wildlife. Ronnie knew otherwise, and planned the new forest with such originality, leaving plenty of open space, and putting in hardwood trees along the burn-sides, that his critics were confounded. When the project began, there were no more than a dozen roe deer in the whole area. Thirty years later the population had risen to some 9000, in spite of an annual cull of over 1,000. The explosion of birds was equally spectacular. Pessimists had predicted that the forest would contain no bird-life, but today over 300 species have been counted – an immense increase over the few that struggled for a living on the bare grassland before.

To go out with Ronnie at dawn into the forest, and hear his commentary on every animal or bird that moved or called, was a rare privilege. I particularly cherish his account of how he pressed a colony of short-eared owls into service as auxiliary warriors in a campaign against water-voles. The little rodents were burrowing into the wall of a dam which he had just built to make a new pond, and threatening to collapse it. The owls were established about six hundred yards up the valley. Knowing their predilection for alighting on posts, Ronnie hammered in some fence-posts, and by gradually moving them down and down, lured the owls into the target area, where they made short work of the voles and saved the dam.

A short, stocky man, who never lost his Deeside accent – it was always 'frae thess' and 'tae thart' – he was volcanically articulate, and in retirement became a highly valued spokesman for the Scottish Gamekeepers' Association, bitterly condemning the wholesale massacres of deer organised by the Deer Commission (Scotland), the Forestry Commission and the National Trust for Scotland. So powerful were his contributions to hearings in the Scottish Assembly in Edinburgh, such was his good sense, that when he bore down on the capital to castigate the members for their ignorance of country matters, it was said you could see them pouring out through the back door of their £430-million building like rats leaving a sinking ship.

Alas, his splendid voice is now muted, for in 2005 he was partially disabled by a stroke. But his great creation at Eskdalemuir will live on, and he will be remembered by it.

Another outstanding companion on the hill was James Teacher, known to friends as 'Teach', for years Joint Master of the Quorn, and part-owner of Fealar, the high-lying forest that marches with Atholl. A forceful character and a keen practical joker, he was also a knowledgeable ecologist, an excellent writer and a philanthropist rolled into one. Although he employed professsional stalkers, he liked nothing better than to go out on his own at Fealar with a pony-man in attendance – and he was on one of his solitary forays when he saw three men come over the ridge out of the neighbouring forest. There were stags lying some 300 yards on his side of the march, but the intruders, after a good look round, crossed the boundary and started to stalk them.

Had Teach fired or shot, or just let out a yell, he could have scared off both the men and the deer. Instead, he lay low in the heather and watched as a successful stalk went in and one of the party shot a stag. Having gralloched it and tied a white handkerchief to a marker stick, the trio withdrew over the skyline, presumably to fetch their pony or an Argo.

Seconds after they had disappeared, Teach was up on a high knollie signalling up his pony-man. He then ran across to the dead stag, dragged it down to the bottom of the corrie, helped load it on to the saddle and sent it away to the larder. Then he ran back up the face, kicked the gralloch into a hole under some heather and moved the marker-stick with its flag to a similar brae a couple of hundred yards along the shoulder.

With that he slipped away and awaited events, relishing the thought that the poachers must have been dumbfounded when they discovered that their gut-less stag had upped and vanished. Nothing happened for three days, but then a message came through on the radio: the opposition had shot a stag on the march and lost it. Had Fealar any news of it? Alas, Teach replied: nothing to report. For twenty years or more the intruders remained baffled. Then at last a brief account of the incident appeared in the sporting press, and, if they saw it, their bewilderment must have turned at last to mortification

Yet another magnetically enthusiastic deer man is Paul Wood, manager of the Screebe estate in Connemara, in the far west of Ireland, where, over the past dozen years, he has presided over an extraordinary development. The last native red deer in the area were shot out during the famines of the 1840s, but now a new race has taken over their former territory, with amazing results.

Reintroductions began in 1996, when a German entrepreneur, Nikolai Burkart, owner of the Screebe estate, imported sixteen red deer from a farm in Co. Wexford. Deriving originally from the herds in Windsor Great Park and Warnham Park, the young animals were of excellent pedigree, but nobody foresaw how phenomenally well they would do in their new environment. The terrain looks unpromising, and not unlike that of Letterewe, consisting largely of rock and water, with the mountains rising to 3,000 feet, and annual rainfall measured in feet rather than inches; yet the newcomers grew at an astonishing rate.

Soon Paul began to see stags with only their second heads carrying fourteen points – as many as an Imperial in Scotland – and when they reached maturity several had more than thirty points. The most remarkable of all – a beast known as The Pirate, because he had lost one eye – carried forty-four points in his prime. Weights also became enormous: one stag called The Sailor was so massive that when he was culled a team of seven men with a quad bike could not extract his carcase, and had to quarter him where he fell. In the larder his aggregated weight came out at 700 lbs, or fifty stone – three times the weight of a good Scottish stag.

What causes this phenomenal growth? Paul believes the secret lies in the conifer plantations belonging to Coillte, the Irish State forestry organisation. Luckily for the deer, these woods are not fenced, so that they provide ideal feeding and shelter. Most red deer are grazers, but regular analysis of droppings has shown that the Screebe animals are predominantly browsers, and that the main ingredients of their diet are bramble leaves and willow. Grass scarcely features in their diet, because there is so little available: only a few small fields are scattered about among the rock and bog. Experts believe that one reason for the exceptional build-up of bone in body and antler is the high mineral content of the herbage, deriving from the underlying limestone.

Fortunately Herr Burkart runs the estate as an ecological experiment, rather than for commercial gain, and so has no difficulty resisting the blandishments of trophy-hunters who would give anything to shoot one of the giants. For several years the master stag was a massive animal known from his aggressive behaviour as The Mugger, and during the rut of 2004 he proved a severe temptation to a visiting American who had negotiated to shoot a good stag, but not one of the top flight. Day after day, when Paul took the American out, they saw the monster, and time and again the visitor offered $20,000 to shoot him, but Burkart was determined that the head of his foundation stag should remain at Screebe. In the end he told the American that he might shoot The Mugger for nothing, provided he left the trophy behind – and the American declined.

All the same, the time came when the two leading stags had both passed their prime. Paul shot The Mugger when he was clearly losing condition, and it turned out that he had had one kidney pulped in a fight. Burkart himself accounted for The Pirate, knowing that the great beast had passed on his genes to his offspring. Both their tremendous sets of antlers now adorn the walls of the lodge at Screebe, testimony to the exceptional adaptability that deer possess. In 2007 the proprietor's enterprise in bringing them back to Connemara was amply rewarded, when the *Conseil International de la Chasse* – the authority which adjudicates on such matters – confirmed that The Pirate had set a new British and Irish record for a wild red deer head.

I have never spent a day on the hill with a stalker I did not like. I have always found it a joy to be in the company of professional hill-men, to observe how they move and analyse the constantly changing situation, to share their knowledge of the deer and the environment, and to hear about their own lives. I remember no more stimulating companion than Sandy Masson, with whom I went out at Dougarie, on the Isle of Arran, and who later became Head Stalker at Balmoral. One morning, after several other manoeuvres had been frustrated, we stalked and shot what Sandy thought was a fairly young stag with a spindly head, but when we went up to it, he let out a long groan of *'Oh, oh, oh, oh!'* and hung his jacket over its head in a mock-serious attempt to conceal its antlers. If he had realised from a distance that it was a 13-pointer, he would never have let me shoot it – but in fact it had a very small head, more of a freak than a trophy.

Another freak on Arran in those days was Whitey, a pure white stag with only one antler, who lived to be fifteen or sixteen, in spite of being dangerously conspicuous and showing up like a beacon on the hill. All his life he was a social outcast, rejected by the rest of the herd, no doubt because of his colour, and he never produced any white off-spring – but he reminded me of the famous white hind of Loch Treig, which was supposed to have lived for nearly 200 years in the seventeenth and eighteenth centuries. Not knowing that a Highland deer could live for only twenty years at most, one land-owner after another failed to realise that what they were seeing was a succession of white ladies, each probably the daughter of its predecessor. I am sorry to say that Whitey himself came to a bad end, shot in the village at Lochranza, where he had taken to flipping the lids off dustbins and foraging among the contents.

All the forests in which I have stalked remain vivid in my mind, and all have to some extent survived. Loch Choire, to which we have returned several times as guests of our friend Val Fleming, remains inimitably beautiful, although the number of stags it carries has diminished sharply, and the grouse have practically gone – the result of the keepers not being allowed to burn the heather. The most cheerful feature (from our point of view) is a living link with the past, in the form of Ronnie Macdonald, who came to the forest in one of our early years (as I have related), and is there to this day as second stalker, a bit heavier, a bit slower (thank goodness), but still incomparably cheerful, and the best possible fun.

As everywhere in Sutherland, the Loch Choire deer suffered badly in the savage winter of 2009-10, and although the estate put out generous amounts of hay, nuts and mineral blocks, at least 150 died: moreover, many hinds aborted or absorbed their calves, so that the herd was much reduced.

One morning in the autumn of 2010, high on the flank of Meall Cailleach – the hill of the witch – our party was moving cautiously forward into the blast of a roaring south-east wind. We had spied shootable stags ahead of us, and were working round a steep face to get above them when one of us suddenly suddenly spotted a single antler sticking up over the skyline, no more than forty yards above us, to our right. Quickly Ronnie pulled the rifle out of its cover, slid a round into the breach and settled Ian, the shooter that day, into a firing position, with the barrel canted upwards at an angle of seventy degees. The rest of us crouched against the hill, hardly daring to lift our heads.

The ground was so steep that we could see no more of the beast than that one antler, outlined against a succession of hurtling clouds and patches of blue sky, and these gave the impression that the head was moving. For minute after minute we watched it through binoculars – and if we turned to look out over Corrie na Fearn and Loch Choire itself, the racing, pewter-coloured cloud shadows assumed fantastical shapes as they fled up over distant faces: one moment a perfect outline of Ireland was speeding up Corrie Ba, and then a gigantic, crouching rabbit appeared on the lower slopes of Meall an Eoin, only to melt within seconds into a ragged blur as it travelled rapidly uphill.

Tense with anticipation, we waited. The temptation was to give a whistle and bring the stag to its feet; but the odds were that, if we made the slightest sound, with one bound it would be gone, giving Ian no chance of a shot. So we waited. But after quarter of an hour Ronnie and I had begun to harbour the same suspicion and were muttering to each other, 'Are you sure this bugger isn't dead?' Would any live deer lie as still as this? We waited some more, then climbed cautiously towards the skyline, to discover that we had been stalking the skeleton of a winter casualty – a mature seven-pointer. There was something spooky about those remains, lying on a little shelf high above the glen. The head and rib-cage were more or less intact, and some rough hair still clung to the neck; but the leg-bones had been scattered by scavengers, and all the soft tissue had gone. Back at the lodge, Ronnie did his best to keep the episode under wraps; but word inevitably got out, causing tremendous hilarity in the gun-room. An experienced hill-man stalking a dead stag? How ridiculous! But in fact he had done everything by the book.

The incident recalled the story of a pompous Victorian gentleman who fancied his prowess on the hill, and began the day by informing his stalker and ghillie that he would lead the party: they were to follow him, and not to speak unless spoken to. Only if he asked them a question were they to volunteer an opinion. In the morning all went well, and he shot a stag. He then had his piece and carried on – but in the afternoon things proved less satisfactory. He walked for miles, lost his bearings, and for hours saw nothing – until at last he spotted the antlers of a stag lying behind a rock. A quick stalk put the party within range, and the gentleman lay ready in a firing position ... but the minutes dragged by, and in the end, irritated beyond further endurance, he turned and whispered angrily to the stalker: 'This stag's an awful long time rising.' To which the stalker replied, 'Aye, he will be verra long arising, because he's dead.' The expert had stalked the stag he had shot in the morning.

Often in recent years Ronnie has designated me relief Argo driver and given me instructions to slip back, fetch the vehicle, and bring it round to the bottom of the next glen while the rest of the party go in over the top. Once he left an Argo parked at the top of a dizzyingly steep grass slope, and when he asked me to go back for it, gave me some quick advice about how to manage the descent. 'If she starts to go,' he said ... but somehow I failed to take in the rest of the instruction. No sooner was I rolling, pointing downwards so steeply that I was almost lying on the windscreen, when she did start to go, sliding and accelerating horribly. Every instinct said 'Brake! Brake!', but I knew that might be disastrous, and somehow in the last possible second I remembered Ronnie's other phrase, 'Give her a burst'. One quick twitch of the hand-throttle put more power into the wheels and re-established their grip on the turf – but it was a close-run thing.

A similar commission came on an afternoon of surpassing heat. The stalking party was on its way home, working down on to the Whip, and Ronnie asked me to take the Argo back to the foot of the hill, near the loch. From that point I kept watch for a while, but, having seen nothing, and feeling excessively hot, I stripped off on a little beach and went for a swim, forging up and down alongside my Labrador Jemima. Then, as I waded back to land through the shallows, I suddenly realised that there were deer within about 300 yards, with a good-sized stag among them. I was just thinking, 'Why the hell don't they stop messing about on the hill, and come down and shoot this fellow?' when, as I was towelling-off, a shot cracked out from close at hand, and the stag fell down dead. Hastily pulling on clothes and boots, I leapt into the Argo and drove the short distance to the body – to find, of course, that for the last half hour the stalkers had been creeping down the hill towards me, watching my every movement through telescopes and binoculars. 'Fine figure of a man!' Ronnie kept repeating – derisively, I thought – but when Albert Grant, the Head Stalker, heard about the incident, he was more forthright, and began muttering oaths about the place having become a nudist colony.

The great hills of Knoydart are as steep and rugged as ever, but after many vicissitudes and changes of ownership the central part of the estate – 17,000 acres – now belongs to several different owners: the Knoydart Foundation, formed in 1999 (a partnership of local residents), the Highland Council, the Chris Brasher Trust, the Kilchoan estate and the John Muir Trust. There is still no road access from the interior, and vehicles have to come in by sea from Mallaig; but The Old Forge, classed by the *Guinness Book of Records* as the remotest pub in mainland Britain, has nine moorings, an excellent menu, and a collection of 'resident fiddles' and other instruments for impromptu music-making. Glenfeshie has also changed hands several times, and Tony Dulverton (who died in 1992) would be both agonised and infuriated if he knew about the massacre of 2004. He would have been the first to point out the futility of mass-murder on that scale – for whenever a vacuum is created, deer pour into it from the surrounding forests.

Glenkinglass has remained marvellously unchanged. The river estuary has been bridged, the road up the glen improved, and new barns have been built behind the lodge; but when I walked over from Black Mount recently, I found the little house exactly as I remembered it twenty years earlier, with the log-box still firmly anchored to the wall in the porch. The hills look just as steep, and although Tim Healy has retired, after thirty years on the estate, I feel sure that the wee folk still haunt the bridge at Acharn. It is sad that Lorna Schuster, who went to the hill (albeit in an Argo) at the age of ninety-six, died at last in 2009.

Conaglen remains in the Guthries' safe hands, and neighbouring Glenaladale still belongs to Hugh Cheape, who recently demonstrated the strength of his attachment to the forest by replacing the Colt wooden bungalow with a handsome, two-storey lodge built of stone and slate. Davy is still the stalker there, and when he discovered the only spot on the estate where it was possible to get a mobile telephone signal, he built a cairn and brilliantly named it Carn a Voda (phone). So far as I know, the binoculars which I lost coming down from the Gaskan flats are still lying somewhere in the face. I have told Davy that if he finds them, he can have them; yet he too has always searched in vain. One summer some careless canoeists set fire to the whole hillside, burning out 1,000 acres, so that unless the glasses fell into a deep hollow, the rubber covering and eye-pieces have probably been destroyed and the lenses cracked. Whatever state they are in, nothing short of an earthquake is likely to reveal them now.

At Corrour, also, the wooden lodge has gone, replaced by a grandiose castle of steel and glass, built by the Rausing family, owners of the Tetra Pak drinks carton business. Trains still stop at the railway halt, but the Station House no longer welcomes walk-in ducks and geese. Rather, it has become a restaurant, café and pub. The little lodge at Strathossian looks much the same from a distance – though a good deal smartened – but the inside has been done up out of all recognition, with a fully fitted kitchen, central heating, television, telephone, double-bedroom and en-suite bathroom (ye gods!) on the ground floor, another bathroom upstairs, more bedrooms ... but no dispensation, I imagine, for hanging roe deer on the back of bedroom doors. Geordie Nairn lives in retirement at Fersit, dismayed to see how much deer stocks have diminished on the hill which he managed with such care.

Letterewe has probably changed less than any of the other forests. The lodge at Carnmore has been refurbished, and I daresay that on stormy nights it does not talk as loudly as it used to. But, thanks to Paul's determination, and his expenditure, one of Britain's last great wildernesses remains intact, and the forest is still in the hands of his family. His plan to reintroduce wolves never came to fruition, but the idea has been revived by Paul Lister, proprietor of the Alladale estate, who has already imported elk and wild boar, and hopes eventually to bring in lynx and brown bears as well as wolves, as part of his ambitious scheme to re-establish the Highlands' ancient fauna.

In the south, when we moved house from Oxfordshire to Gloucestershire, I had to bid farewell to my old haunts; but all the estates on which I worked remain intact, and the deer in Stonor Park are still flourishing. Not so the Nepalese monarchy. Both King Birendra and Prince Dhirendra, for whom I had ghillied in the snow, were murdered in the massacre of June 2001, when, crazed by drugs and alcohol, Crown Prince Dipendra gunned down ten members of his own family, including himself, and in effect put an end to the dynasty. But I am glad to say that Hemanta Mishra has established himself as a leading conservationist in America.

In the Cotswolds I was lucky enough to find a new stalking beat at Miserden, the 3000-acre estate of Tom Wills. Once again the main species of deer were (and are) the fallow, which move up and down a long valley and over the fields from their stronghold in Cirencester Park. There are also a few roe, and a growing number of muntjac. The landscape is more dramatic than that of the Chilterns, with steeper slopes and deeper valleys, but the mixture of farm and deciduous woodland is much the same.

So is the challenge of trying to achieve a responsible cull – and even now, nearly fifty years after I started, I am still fascinated by the deer. Every time I go out, I feel there is a chance of seeing some new facet of their behaviour – as happened on a fine winter morning when the bucks had settled back into all-male groups after the rut.

The sun had just cleared the horizon as I came up through a larch wood into beautiful little grass bowl, with a four-foot high dry-stone wall running round the far side of it. In the bowl seven deer were grazing – three great bucks, two sorels and two prickets. The sun, streaming low across them from the right, brought out the dark winter colours of their coats and flashed off their antlers when they moved their heads. As I watched, the prickets began idly sparring, shoving at each other with their short spikes – but then I saw an interloper heading their way.

Trotting towards them along the top of the wall came a big dog fox, splendidly illuminated, red in the jacket, white on the throat. One of the prickets, spotting him, faced up and began to make jabbing movements with his head. The fox, which was just about on the level of the deer's ears, stopped and began to thrash its brush back and forth. When the pricket went even closer and took a few more jabs, it sat down and gave the deer a look which I swear was condescending and said, in effect, 'Bad luck, mate – you'll never get me.' Then it got up again and walked on, quite leisurely – whereupon both prickets moved briskly along the wall below it, giving little skips and shaking their heads.

Alas, the tableau suddenly crumbled when a treacherous eddy of wind came round behind me. One of the old stagers whipped up his head and bolted, putting the whole group to flight. With a final flourish of its brush the fox flipped down the far side of the wall, and in a few seconds all the players had vanished. I was left wishing I had had a camera – but what a way to start the morning.

Acknowledgements

I wish I could salute all the people who have contributed to my love and understanding of deer – but many of them are no longer here to be thanked. Prominent among departed mentors are John Barstow, Tony, Lord Dulverton, John Gassman, Ron LeVay, Raoul Millais, John Schuster, James Teacher and Paul van Vlissingen.

The living – to all of whom I am much indebted – include Denis Bergin, Jock Cairney, John Crosthwaite-Eyre, Robin Fleming, Val Fleming, Sir Max Hastings, Tim Healy, Ray Jenkins, Donald Kennedy, David Lyon, Davy McAuley, Dr Archie McDiarmid, Ken McDiarmid, Tony Marsh, Steven McKenzie, Robin Maclean, Hemanta Mishra, George Nairn, Ronnie Macdonald, Dicky Michel von Tüssling, Chris Ogilvie, Steve Poole, Ronnie Rose, Dougie Russell, Hans Schleifenbaum, Pat Synnott, Sir Michael Wigan, Freddie Wills, Tom Wills and Paul Wood. I am particularly grateful to Hugh Cheape, for providing translations of Gaelic names, and to the stalker-historian Iain Thornber for the generosity with which he shares ideas, information and photographs, on and off the hill.

Index